THE GOWER STREET POLTERGEIST

By the same author

INVASION 1940

★

BRAZILIAN ADVENTURE

ONE'S COMPANY

NEWS FROM TARTARY

A FORGOTTEN JOURNEY

★

A STORY TO TELL

THE SIXTH COLUMN

MY AUNT'S RHINOCEROS

WITH THE GUARDS TO MEXICO!

The Gower Street Poltergeist

PETER FLEMING

RUPERT HART-DAVIS
Soho Square London
1958

Printed in Great Britain by Richard Clay and Company, Ltd.,
Bungay, Suffolk

CONTENTS

ACKNOWLEDGMENTS

These essays, or whatever you like to call them, have all appeared in the *Spectator*, under the pseudonym of Strix. I am grateful to the Editor for permission to republish them.

PETER FLEMING

Nettlebed, Oxfordshire

THE TWO SAFES

THE man I am thinking of now used to be in the Secret Service. Let us call him B. The point about B was that he had a safe; and now I have a safe, too. Though the purposes for which they were manufactured were similar if not necessarily identical, these two receptacles seem to have little in common, and this is a source of disappointment to me.

B's safe did not, of course, belong to him, any more than a battleship belongs to her captain; B's safe belonged to King George V. Mine, on the other hand, is my own property; it was given to me by my mother about six months ago. In some families such a gift might seem odd, but not in ours. Only last week she gave me a saddle, a wardrobe, some trays for storing apples on and several small planks; one of my brothers got a coal-scuttle and a pair of ski-ing sticks. The fact is that my mother is rather restless. However tight the housing situation may be, she always seems to own several large houses. They are never, unfortunately, the houses that she really wants to own, so after a time she unloads them one by one on to the market, acquiring other, and in the long run equally undesired, residences in their place.

This (as far as we can see) endless process results in periodical windfalls for my brothers and myself. Each time the property-market reels to our mother's latest body-blow, a shower of débris descends upon us: nursery fenders, water-softeners, chicken-coops, barometers, towel-horses, sundials, croquet sets. It would not be true to say that a majority, or even a large minority, of these movables fulfil in our own households anything that might be described as a long-felt want. But they are

7

movables, and when our mother says that if nobody takes them away they will only be left for those awful people—a term invariably applied to the charming and intelligent couple ("he says he was at school with you") with whom she opened negotiations several weeks ago— we generally give in with a good grace. It was the sale of No. 22 which produced the coal-scuttle and the trays for storing apples on; the safe came my way when she disposed of the Abbey last summer.

B's title to his safe may have been less secure, less personal than mine, but it was a very much larger safe. It stood, glum and significant, in a corner of his office, and in the summer, I seem to remember, a portable electric fan whirred and weaved to and fro on top of it. Though you could hear traffic charging along the waterfront, and though beyond that the big ships and the little craft on the wide river honked and whistled at each other, making rather the same intermittent pattern of sound that you get when geese and widgeon are feeding together, B's office was a quiet place. Occasionally a hawker passed down the narrow street in which it stood, crying his wares in a harsh fatalistic sing-song. If this impersonal noise, meaningless to most foreigners, asserted itself at the right moment, B would stop talking (if you were talking, which was on the whole unlikely, he would hold up his hand, say "Sorry, just a second . . ." and stare abstractedly over your head). "War *wee* bor *shu-u-u-ng!*" (or words to that effect) the hawker would yell with a kind of casual but at the same time emphatic despair. B would relax with a small, rueful smile. "Not for me," he would say, on a note of humorous apology, if this was the first time he had tried this gambit on you. But once he was sure that you understood his little pantomime he would give a subtler, less obvious performance; only a very slight cocking of his head, a narrowing of his eyes, an unwonted hesitation in his speech let you see that he was expecting some secret message to reach him from the teeming and perilous world outside.

I don't suppose that B, as an officer engaged on secret duties, could have done without his safe; as an actor (which is what he really was, though no one paid him for it) he certainly found it invaluable. It was a stage property on which he could place complete reliance. Telephone calls from the Ambassador's secretary, from Naval Intelligence, from Military Intelligence and from B's girl-friend were not indeed infrequent, but that was about the best you could say for them. The purpose of the Ambassador's secretary was generally to postpone, and that of B's girl-friend to demand, an interview; Naval and Military Intelligence normally rang up only to ask B where on earth he had got the information he sent them yesterday.

But the safe was an ally—a familiar, almost—of a completely dependable kind. B's office was bare, spruce and impersonal, and calculated, therefore, to disappoint a visitor whose preconceived ideas about the Secret Service were in any way romantic. There was a map on the wall, but it was a perfectly ordinary map which had abandoned several years ago its pretensions to up-to-dateness. B, as he paced up and down, speaking with much cogency of trends, of forces at work, of repercussions and destinies and stresses, of *ballons d'essai* and of spheres of interest, would occasionally stop in front of it. "You see what I mean?" he would say. "It's *these* people who've got the ball at their feet now." And his long thin actor's hand would reach up and spreadeagle itself upon several hundred square miles of territory. "If they move—I say *if* they move—they won't go North. Oh, no. They'll come down *this* way." And his

9

hand would sweep with dramatic and inexorable sudden-
ness down the map.

But the map itself was not really important. Like an
actor's sword, it was not intended for use, but only to
make certain types of gesture feasible and effective. The
safe played a much less negative part. In addition to
liking the sound of his own voice, B had a very real gift
of exposition. He talked at length, but he talked in a
clear and persuasive way and was easy to listen to; so it
happened more often than not that when one rose to
leave, the morning or the afternoon (as the case might be)
was far advanced. "Wait half a second," B would say,
"and we'll go along together." A few deft, decisive
gestures would straighten out his far from disorderly
desk. Then he would walk across to the safe and unlock
it (an intricate process), walk back, pick up the wastepaper-basket, put it in the safe and shut the massive door
with a muted but portentous clonk.

"Sorry to keep you waiting," he would say. "Let's go."

I don't know what it was about this little bit of by-
play that was so impressive. It reminded one that however freely he had been talking—and B always gave you
the impression that he was telling you all, and indeed
often rather more than, he knew—his duties involved
him in darker, more clandestine mysteries to which you
could never be privy; and it also conjured up, by implication, a vivid sense of the ubiquity and enterprise of B's
enemies, whose agents were liable to effect, by stealth or
violence, an entry into his office while he was out to
luncheon and wrest from his casual, unregarded jottings
clues of a capital importance. One might not have—
indeed, to be frank, one never had—formed a tremendous-
ly high opinion of B while he was talking to one; but when
he stopped talking, and in unaccustomed silence stowed
his wastepaper-basket into the safe, one couldn't help feel-

ing that there must be a good deal more to the man than one had realised.

I do not say that I had planned to use my mother's safe to induce in my fellow-men a truer, or anyhow a higher, appreciation of my own intrinsic worth. But whenever I look at it I remember B's safe with a certain envy, and am saddened by the thought of how little comparable value I am getting out of mine. Though it is small—smaller, actually, than my wastepaper-basket—it is just too big for its position between the bookcase and the door, so that the children contuse themselves upon it when they come in and I bark my shins on it when I go out. It has the advantage of being, apart from myself, the only thing in the room that the puppy has not partially destroyed by chewing; but it does not even begin to do for me the things that B's safe did for him. I have never impressed anyone by taking out of it (as B once did in my presence) an automatic pistol and slipping it into my pocket or by thrusting into it with an air of *empressement* a bundle of intriguing-looking documents. What is more, I know beyond all possible doubt that I shall never do either of these things or anything remotely like them: unless, when my mother once more changes her abode, she happens to come across the key.

VIPERS LONG AGO

THERE are hardly any snakes in the part of England where I live, and when I was a boy I regretted this very much. I was keen on snakes. In retrospect it seems likely that my choice of this aberrant hobby was in part due to a desire to be different. At my private school the two recognised things to "collect" were birds' eggs and butterflies. What might be described as the Bullingdon

11

set went in for birds' eggs; the dimmer, worthier boys collected butterflies. I collected snakes.

Besides the desire to *épater*, illegality added a certain relish to this pursuit; for we were not unnaturally forbidden to have anything to do with the adders which were fairly common in that region of Dorset. Apart, however, from these unworthy impulses snakes really did have a fascination for me. They are extremely beautiful creatures. A grass-snake swimming in clear water is a sight at once infinitely graceful and mildly mysterious; and in the spring, when it has sloughed its old skin and the black zigzag down its spine shows up against silvery green scales, an adder coiled on sunlit turf is none the less lovely for being sinister at the same time.

My mania, which absorbed most of my spare time during the summer terms, expressed itself in two ways: I kept grass-snakes, and I killed adders and skinned them. I usually had three or four grass-snakes at a time. They lived in an old playbox and were fed at irregular intervals with frogs and also, I am sorry to say, with nestlings taken from the hedges. These hapless creatures were left in the playbox and, although the snakes took no interest in them while one was watching, by the next morning they had vanished and the circumference of one or more of the snakes had increased.

Snakes, I soon discovered, are not much help if you want to win friends and influence people. When, at the Parents' Cricket Match in my first year, I proudly produced my favourite serpent for inspection by my mother, even I could not help noticing a certain lack of true rapture in her exclamations of delight; nor did I fail to mark the looks of horror and disgust from the Mums in adjacent deck-chairs, as Ponto, his forked tongue flickering, was put through his paces by his young master.

But the universal unpopularity of my dumb friends

was not always a dead loss. Once, travelling home for the holidays, I decided that the most efficient way of transporting snakes on (so to speak) the hoof was to carry them in my sponge-bag, a handy receptacle in which I could at a moment's notice satisfy myself as to their welfare. The journey was a long one, the train crowded. There came a moment when, glancing upwards at the rack, I saw that the snakes had made a bid for freedom and were undulating with their usual air of clueless but dignified composure above the heads of the passengers opposite. Muttering apologies, I recaptured them. Character-building is perhaps the best epithet with which to describe the experience of putting, at the age of eleven, three grass-snakes into one sponge-bag in a railway compartment full of angry adults; but after the next stop we had the carriage to ourselves.

Killing adders was the nearest one could get to big-game hunting at that age. They never, in my experience, attacked, but when cornered they struck fiercely at the stick you were whacking at them with, and you felt at times uneasily aware of your bare legs and gym-shoes. Moreover they were not plentiful or easy to surprise; they generally lay coiled up on the edge of a patch of brambles or gorse or near a pile of rocks. Stealth and speed were needed to intercept them before they slithered into cover.

Snakes are the easiest of all animals to skin. You simply slit them down the belly with a pair of scissors and peel them like a banana; then you tack the skin on to a board to dry and rub alum into it. Early in the summer an adder-skin is a pretty thing. But soon the silvery-green changes to pale yellow or pale olive green and after that gets steadily darker, so that the smart black zigzag markings merge into it and by August most adders look drab and unremarkable.

It was probably pride rather than filial piety which made me send my first skin home as a present to my mother. She professed herself delighted with it and in a rash moment wrote that she was having it made into a *bandeau*, a circlet-like arrangement with which at that period ladies sometimes bound their tresses. Dimly apprehending that women like to have several different specimens of the same thing (such as a hat or a skirt) to choose from, I sent her more adder-skins.

Summer terms last a long time. Perhaps the skins faded, or stank; perhaps the fashion changed. At any rate, when we were at length reunited, I observed with chagrin that my mother's brows were not bound with the spoils of the chase; and though I seem to remember that she did once put the *bandeau* on for my benefit, it was clear that my contributions to her wardrobe had not been of a fundamental nature.

I had a friend who used to come adder-hunting with me, and we formed the ambition—which, though common among big-game hunters today, was not so then —to take a photograph of our quarry. It was quite difficult to get near enough to an adder to hit it with a stick; it proved quite impossible to take a photograph of it with what I think was called a Box Brownie. So after much thought, and not without twinges of our artistic conscience, we decided that the only thing to do was to abandon all hope of photographing an adder in its natural surroundings and to get one to pose (as it were) for us in a place from which it could not escape. The obvious choice for this *venue* was the squash-court.

By this time we had reached a fairly high standard of addermanship. It was not long before we managed to pin one down with a forked stick, although it had been rather battered in the process. I got hold of it just behind the head and we carried it back to the school; for

14

the last lap of the journey, across the playing-fields, we could be seen by authority, and I had to stuff the adder, still clutched convulsively by the throat, into my pocket.

By the time we reached the squash-court the unfortunate adder was in a bad way. It curled itself morosely up in the corner where we put it down and we duly took a photograph of it with the Box Brownie. When this was developed its subject was seen to be indistinguishable from a cowpat. After that we gave up trying to photograph snakes.

THE WINDOWLESS WALL

"GREEDY swine!"

"Greedy swine yourself."

"*Tu quoque* is the sign of a fool, so you must be a fool as well as a swine."

I suppose the verbal sword-play of the schoolroom still includes this classic riposte; and I agree that *tu quoque* is rather a feeble dialectical gambit (though Heaven knows how they would get on without it in the House of Commons). But there is one context in which it hardly ever seems to be used, and I can never quite understand why.

For several decades the Communists have been proclaiming that all non-Communist political systems are doomed; and although not everybody has accepted this forecast, very few people—and those mostly extremists of one sort or another—have suggested that things are at least as likely to work out the other way round.

Only three things can be said, with the precision required of a lexicographer, about Communism. The first is that it is a political doctrine. The second is that it was evolved by persons who were in exile at the time

to approve of at the moment); and anyone's estimate of its future must largely depend on how long he believes that large numbers of his fellow men will continue to rally to a doctrine which, because of its inherent contempt for truth, stands revealed at frequent intervals as nonsensical and base.

Is Communism a wall of the room in which mankind lives? Or is it a monkey-puzzle which has grown up, on what used to be the lawn, during the last half-century and which, after darkening the windows of another generation or two, will fall to the axe or to decay? Although there is almost no limit to the extent to which men's, and especially children's, minds can be abused in a modern totalitarian State, I nevertheless believe that the human animal has, in the long run, the same fundamental need for truth that it has for salt. So I, personally, would plump for the monkey-puzzle, though I doubt if I shall be there to count the rings on its stump.

MURDER IN THE GLENS

IT is a well-established literary convention that the poacher is a sympathetic character. People who write about the country invest him with a raffish glamour and credit him with many primitive skills in taking game and a Robin Hood-like resource in outwitting gamekeepers and police. "Old Simon gave me a scarcely perceptible wink as he slipped out of the bar with his lurcher at his heels. The full moon, I remembered, would be rising about now. . . ." How many times have we read sentences like that?

Good old Simon! Or should it perhaps be good olde Simon? So conveniently picturesque a figure would be a sad loss to rustic *belles lettres*, but does he in fact exist any more, this lone, *rusé*, clandestine hunter threading the moonlit rides? Here and there he may; but most modern poachers are motorised townsmen, operating in impersonal gangs, using a smash-and-grab technique and running very little risk of being caught. They do not favour literary gentlemen with scarcely perceptible winks, and for my part I do not find them estimable or sympathetic.

The only poacher who hardly ever gets written about is the deer-poacher. He is not a picturesque figure. Some idea of his standard methods may be gained from the latest report of the Nature Conservancy.

"The most serious incident during the year took place on the Beinn Eighe Nature Reserve where deer-poaching still continues, despite the vigilance of the Reserve Warden, Mr. J. Polson, and the local Police Constable. On 23rd March, 1955, at about 3.45 a.m. shots were heard on the Reserve and a car was shortly afterwards intercepted. Two men were in the car, one describing himself as a farm worker and the other as a gamekeeper. In the rear were two stags, one on top of the other. The one on top had eight bullets in it—two in the haunch, three through the stomach, one through the lung, one through the nose and one through the antler. This stag was dead. The one underneath had had one bullet through the right eye passing between the brain and the roof of the mouth. It was still alive nearly an hour after being shot, but paralysed, and was put out of its misery by the warden. One of the men was charged and convicted under the Firearms Act, 1937, and the Games Licences Act, 1860, and fined £10 on the first charge and £15 on the second. The other was convicted under the latter Act only and was fined £15. . . . For one of the men this was the second conviction in three years and for the other man, the third conviction within the same period. . . . It is difficult to estimate what is the value of a stag to a poacher, but somewhere in the region of £10 would seem a reasonable estimate, and on that assumption the fines levied approximately equalled double the value of the two stags in this case."

On this jolly incident the following comments may be made. First, the only unusual thing about it was that the poachers were caught. Second, nothing was or could be said about the number of deer wounded but not recovered during the shooting; the deer are generally in a herd when fired on and casualties of this kind are almost always inflicted, especially if the shooting is done at night. Thirdly, the men were not fined because of anything they had done to the deer, but because one of their firearms certificates was not in order and neither of them had game licences.

Bird's-nesting is illegal, but to kill or disable a stag, a hind or even a calf is not in itself an offence. The red deer is the largest wild animal in these islands, but the law does not recognise it as either having a right to or needing protection. Although in many of her overseas possessions the larger mammals are protected by sensible and enlightened game laws, Great Britain is the only civilised country in the world where there is no close season for deer.

There are several interrelated reasons why nothing continues to be done about this minor national disgrace. One is that, although every year more and more people visit the Highlands, hardly any of them ever see the deer. In July, August and September, when public opinion streams along the roads in cars and coaches, the deer look down on it incuriously from two or three thousand feet up; they are not part of the visible land-

20

scape, as ponies are in the New Forest. The result is that good-hearted people, who are quite ready to get hot under the collar about what happens in public to bulls in Spain (where they have never been), remain intellectually and emotionally isolated from what may well be happening this evening to deer on the knoll where they ate their sandwiches last summer.

A more cogent factor is the attitude of an articulate minority of farmers, headed at the moment by the Black-Faced Sheep Breeders' Association. Their case, which is based on specious economics, rooted in shallow ideology and unsupported by any evidence worth hearing, is that deer are vermin, and that a close season, which would probably arrest the decline in their numbers, would do a major disservice to Scottish agriculture; the only gainers would be the beastly people who own deer-forests and a few sentimental cranks.

Since the enemies of the deer greatly outnumber in voting power their friends, the whole business represents what is known as a "delicate" political issue; this means an issue which successive administrations feel they have almost every excuse for funking. But what is done to the deer is abominable and against all our traditions; and it is what is done that matters. I see from its report that last year the Nature Conservancy had some success in preserving in their natural state such items in our heritage as Fossiliferous Mudstones, Green Spleenwort, Bloody Cranesbill, Broad-leaved Ragwort, Marsh Andromeda, the Black Hairsteak, the Chequered Skipper, and some particularly interesting sedge and ling. I am relieved to know that these by-products of Dame Nature stand a good chance of surviving; but I cannot see that, either from a national or an humanitarian point of view, the Broad-leaved Ragwort stands in greater need of conservation than an in-calf hind.

HIGH TEA AT BUCKINGHAM PALACE

It would be a great pity, and quite contrary to the traditions and indeed the interests of our curious society, if nobody ever criticised the Royal Family. The Queen and Prince Philip happen to be (to put it mildly) popular, and to deserve their popularity. But they frequently do things which seem to some of their subjects quite inexcusable: like playing polo on Sunday, being civil (or alternately not civil enough) to Russian statesmen and divorced persons, and appearing with insufficient frequency on television.

But the strong feelings to which these lapses or excesses give rise are mainly of a sectional or sectarian nature; and the attacks launched on the Royal Family, whether editorially or in the correspondence columns of the press, are short-lived, tactical affairs, mere skirmishes. They are uninteresting because they are generally puerile and often have a contrived or exhibitionist air about them. "I am sure I am not the only British mother who feels that Prince Charles is being deprived . . ." You have got to be a pretty good ass to write that sort of letter at all, and a still bigger ass to send it to the *Daily Beast*.

It was accordingly refreshing to read in the *New Statesman* a diatribe conceived in more strategical terms. The strategy was that, as Captain Liddell Hart would put it, of the indirect approach. The anonymous writer began by drawing our shocked attention to an expensive party given at Claridges by a Hungarian for two débutantes; "its splendours were duly communicated to British workers, in goggling detail, by the daily press," he wrote.

I thought at first it was the splendours of the party he was objecting to: not to the press for duly * reporting them, to the detail for goggling, or to the British workers for reading the resultant rubbish. But it soon appeared that these splendours were illusory. "Things," this former *bon vivant* went on, "are not what they used to be." He spoke darkly of bad champagne, dubious caviar and village dressmakers. There is some internal evidence that he lives in a world of his own; but it is a world that gives him cause for disquiet and indignation.

He sums up his misgivings as follows: "Every all-night party, every case of champagne, every hamper † of *pâté de foie gras* is one more proof that the Welfare State no longer exists . . . that equality is not just around the corner but receding into the remote distance."

Whether equality (whatever that means) is receding or not, it seems to be a conception infirmly grasped by the writer in the *New Statesman*, who buttresses his theory that things are not what they used to be with references to the social success achieved by "even minor heiresses from Milwaukee, even junior financiers from Frankfurt, even fourth secretaries from seedy Middle Eastern Embassies." As a frequent reader of the *New Statesman*, I can understand its abhorrence for all heiresses, and particularly those who come from Milwaukee; but surely it is better, and more egalitarian, that the dubious caviar should be sloshed down by minor rather than by major heiresses? I can see, too, that equality, like so many other things, does not apply to foreigners, and that it is

* "*Duly*, adv. Rightly, properly, fitly; sufficiently; punctually." *The Concise Oxford Dictionary*.

† For a brief but (if I may say so) moving account of the uses to which empty *pâté de foie gras* hampers can be put in an emergency, see *Three Weeks in the Sargasso Sea: a Personal Narrative of the Quest for Groundnuts*. By Strix. (Frisby and Beharrel, 21*s*. 1948.) The book is copiously illustrated.

dialectically OK to describe some Middle Eastern Embassies as "seedy," although one cannot help wondering which they are; but again—as in the case of the heiresses —surely there is nothing intrinsically wrong with a fourth secretary, the humblest diplomat on the Embassy staff, getting a whiff of the guilty splendours? Equality would recede still farther if only Ambassadors, and non-seedy ones at that, were asked to these orgies.

In the writer's view the Queen is to blame for all the orgy-mongering that goes on; "one move from the Palace, and the whole complex, hierarchic structure of the Season would collapse." He blames the Royal Family for sponsoring "an outmoded social fashion" which is "at variance with the way of life that most of the Queen's subjects now find admirable."

How on earth this clever chap has discovered which way of life most of the Queen's subjects now find admirable I do not know, and I wish he would write another article and tell us what it is. But meanwhile he points out that the Royal Family "are obliged—if we take the trouble to assert our rights—to do exactly as we tell them." (By "we" I am pretty sure he means the nation, not the *New Statesman*.) He gives royalty credit for being "obliging"; "it pacifies the politicians by pruning down its speeches to the barest bones of platitude: to encourage industry, it daily courts sartorial disaster by patronising English dressmakers." I shouldn't myself have thought that the Queen's clothes were what you might call dowdy, or that Prince Philip's speeches could fairly be described as platitudinous; but this chap, as I say, does rather seem to live in a world of his own.

In his view these perfunctory concessions to "the needs of mid-twentieth-century Britain" are not enough. "The British people are, by now, reconciled to a monarchy whose mental horizons are bounded by Newmarket and Drury Lane; they no longer expect any positive contribution to the welfare of the community; but have they not the right to demand, in return for their annual £75,000, the purely negative virtue of social responsibility?"

He does not say what he means by "social responsibility" nor why he considers it a purely negative virtue; but it is clearly something which he thinks the Royal Family lacks. It is not, at a guess, all that skylarking off to distant parts of the Empire to which he objects; what get him down are "Presentation Parties at Buckingham Palace, Royal Ascot and incessant scurryings between country houses." He would probably not object to the Queen visiting (say) one country house every two months, for the fresh air will do her good; it is the incessant *scurrying* that sets us all such a frightfully bad example. "There will have," he concludes, "to be some big changes at Buckingham Palace when Labour returns to power."

Only one thing in his article disquiets me. He writes: "Is it too much to ask, just once, that the people at the top should set something other than the worst possible example?" I do not like that "just once." It sounds as if we might not be going to get any more of these splendid articles, and I think that would be a very great pity. They make, if I may borrow one of the writer's phrases, "a positive contribution to the welfare of the community."

THE GOWER STREET
POLTERGEIST

THEY tell me (and I am delighted to hear it) that in this issue of the *Spectator* Sir Harold Nicolson is to lead a march-past of the Old Guard; and it has been suggested that I might appropriately give some account of my first tour of duty with the Gower Street Light Infantry. It is a fact, though not a particularly interesting one, that I joined the staff of the *Spectator* when its present editor was five years old; and although my connection with the paper has been interrupted by frequent and sometimes prolonged digressions into other spheres of activity, it goes farther back into the mists of time than anybody else's on the editorial side.

Unfortunately these same mists of time make it a little difficult to remember exactly how this connection began. I spent the winter of 1930–31 in Disraeli's lavatory, working in an honorary capacity for a body called the Economic Advisory Council. I do not know for certain that the narrow little room I occupied had been used as a lavatory by Disraeli when he lived in No. 2 Whitehall Gardens, but it was extraordinarily difficult to imagine what other purpose it could have served. The Economic Advisory Council, which for all I know still exists, heard evidence about and prepared reports on a wide variety of subjects; the three I had most to do with were Conditons in the White Fish Industry, the Education and Supply of Biologists, and the dreaded Tsetse Fly.

The days passed peacefully enough in the great statesman's closet, but I found life on the periphery of the Civil Service unrewarding in more senses than one and when I heard that there would shortly be a vacancy on the staff of the *Spectator* I put myself forward as a candidate. I had never actually read the paper. This is not as surprising as perhaps it sounds. In those days young men (I was twenty-three) were more frivolous than they are now, and the *Spectator*, which sought to edify rather than to entertain, made few concessions to their tastes. Moreover, its circulation—about 21,000—was roughly half of what it is today, and if one was not a subscriber the odds against one coming across a copy were thus twice as high.

In due course I had an interview with J. B. Atkins, an admirable journalist and a delightful, kindly man; it was his impending retirement which would create the vacancy. This was followed by an invitation from Sir Evelyn Wrench to a luncheon at which a series of some twenty articles on the Colour Bar was to be mooted and discussed.

The concept of a series was a popular gimmick of the period, both in journalism and broadcasting; you thought up a challenging theme and then invited a whole string of contributors to give their views on it, thus, in theory, producing a sort of intellectual cliff-hanger and necessitating baton charges to disperse the weekly scrimmages round the bookstalls. I do not, myself, believe that this was how things worked out in practice, but the vogue was well established, and in May, 1931, the first article in the Colour Bar series found itself in double harness with the sixth article in a series called "The Idea of God"; for many weeks thereafter the two ran on and on and on, side by side.

The Colour Bar luncheon took place in what was then the boardroom on a wet, overcast winter's day. As befitted the occasion, a number of coloured races were represented among the distinguished guests. The walls

27

of the boardroom were painted a cultural shade of rather dark sage green, and in the general gloom, though here and there turbans or ebony faces offered badly needed landmarks, it was far from easy to decide whether the man you were talking to was a Parsee or a sallow Member of Parliament, a Cingalese or a swarthy champion of human rights from Columbia University. I found it anxious work.

At the end of the meal Sir Evelyn, after explaining the purpose of our reunion, called upon everyone present to state briefly his views on the Colour Bar. It was not a subject to which at that stage of my career I had devoted a great deal of thought, but it so happened that Mr. Paul Robeson was playing Othello in London at the time, that the Desdemona—Miss Peggy Ashcroft—was and indeed still is a friend of mine, and that in her company I had heard Mr. Robeson say that he was learning German on Linguaphone records: his reason for doing so being that he was fed up with the Colour Bar in America and England and seriously contemplated continuing his artistic career in Germany, the only country whose attitude to racial matters was wholly enlightened and free from prejudice. I reckoned that with the help of this anecdote I could shoot my way out of a tight corner.

Hitler, that winter, was only a bit-player in the *Spectator*'s "News of the Week" paragraphs, and the thesis, lamely advanced when towards nightfall my turn came to speak, that we ought to be thoroughly ashamed of ourselves for being so much less humane than the Germans went down well. Soon afterwards I was offered the job. I broke off relations with the tsetse fly and installed myself (on textual evidence in April, 1931) in a cubicle even smaller than the one I had occupied in Whitehall. This cubicle was, and still is, one of a row which houses most of the editorial staff; "they appear"

28

(I once wrote) "to have been designed either as oubliettes for very minor poets or as ferret-hutches for very large ferrets," and I do not think that this description, though fanciful, is unfair.

It quickly became clear to me that a misleading estimate of my capabilities had been formed by my editorial superiors; this was due, no doubt, to their natural but quite erroneous assumption that I must have had some qualifications for my previous post on the Economic Advisory Council. At that time the first three pages of the paper were taken up with some fifteen or twenty paragraphs summarising the principal events of the week, and when the topics were apportioned I was gravely alarmed to hear the editor saying something like this: "Ah, yes. Electrification of the railways; I see the Weir Committee has reported at last. I expect you'll want to deal with that, Strix. Then this Wheat Conference opens tomorrow—that's up your street, too. And we ought to say something about the Congress of the International Chamber of Commerce in Washington. Again your cup of tea, eh, Strix?"

How I evaded these responsibilities I cannot now remember, but it was soon tacitly recognised that it would be imprudent to extend my scope as a commentator on world affairs beyond the opening of the cricket season, conditions in the white fish industry or revolutions in Latin America. My regular readers, if any such exist, will scarcely be surprised to hear that my first signed book review dealt with a volume called *From Surtees to Sassoon*. Before long I was writing a facetious column (only I don't think they were called columns then) under a pseudonym.

A relaxed and somehow amateurish atmosphere pervaded No. 99 Gower Street in 1931, and it was comparatively easy to introduce such revolutionary innovations as the appointment of a film critic (me). But after four or five months an opportunity presented itself of going to Manchuria, and I asked for leave of absence. When I was half way across Russia Britain went off the gold standard and in the ensuing economic blizzard the *Spectator*'s small staff was drastically reduced.

But they couldn't sack me, because nobody knew where I was. When I returned early in 1932 to the half-empty offices everybody was nonplussed and in the confusion I was appointed Literary Editor. I also became the dramatic critic and wrote a weekly pseudonymous essay. Under the benevolent editorship of Sir Evelyn Wrench, who was often abroad, it was an idyllic existence. Every Tuesday Wilson Harris bounded into the office, produced from his despatch case—like a keeper releasing ferrets from a sack—a leader and a sheaf of paragraphs, and bounded out again. Apart from that the day-to-day running of the paper devolved largely on me, on a charming old man called Wilbraham Cooper, and on Derek Verschoyle, who was then I think twenty-one.

The country-house-cricket atmosphere (at least that is how I remember it) was scarcely ruffled even when one of my essays, entitled "Why Come to Britain?" wiped out, overnight, a whole page of advertisements for hotels and boarding houses. I doubt if anyone has ever got more fun out of periodical journalism at the age of twenty-four. But after a few months another far-fetched enterprise engaged my attention and I vanished once more into the shark-infested jungles.

I have always thought it extremely fortunate for the *Spectator* that I did so.

EVERYBODY ON THE 8.15

"FEELING better?"

The invalid, who had adopted, *mutatis mutandis*, a sphinx-like posture, waggled her behind in an irritable and preoccupied way. An unfinished game of patience, two biscuits, a pencil-sharpener, and a work by Miss Enid Blyton glissaded irresolutely to the floor.

"I am writing my diary," she said severely.

I looked over her shoulder. The day's entry read: "*Got a cof.*"

When you are eight years old, I suppose, a diary is a sort of gadget and as such issues—like scissors, stirrup-leathers, cigarette-lighters, nut-crackers and other arte-facts—an automatic challenge. You want to make it work yourself. And for once you can. You are in control. There is none of the usual nonsense: "Oh, *do* let me!" "But why *can't* I?" "Hurry up, darling, do. Perhaps you'd better let Daddy finish it?" With a diary you have, more or less, *carte blanche*.

The privileges of childhood are many, and the oppor-tunity of keeping a diary is hardly among the most envi-able of them. But it is perhaps the only *unconditional* privilege, not susceptible to curtailment or supervision by higher authority. It is certainly the only privilege of childhood which remains with us, pristine and in-violate, until we die. Yet how many of us do keep diaries?

I cannot answer this question, nor the numerous others contingent on it; but before examining some of the latter it seems only fair to make it clear that I do not keep a diary myself. At one time I used to travel in remote parts of the world, and while doing so I forced myself to keep a sort of log. ("*Jan. 20. V. cold again. Sick camel v. groggy so only did v. short stage. Ate remains of yesterday's hare with noodles. Not much on hare but noodles v. good.*")

The vestigial self-discipline thus acquired—or bequeathed, to be accurate, from my family's rightly totemistic policy towards the entering-up of game-books—failed to survive two sharp rebuffs administered by Fate during the Second World War. Each rebuff was delivered in what can only be described as a pointed manner. On the first occasion, having survived a number of what I regarded as interesting experiences during one of our early retreats, I found myself on the deck of a small boat in the lee of a small island. The boat could not move during daylight for fear of being bombed, and although I was rather tired—a withdrawal (even if orderly, which it seldom is) is the most exhausting of all military operations—I spent the day writing down what had happened in a notebook. An hour before dusk two German bombers on their way home spotted the boat; and that was the end of, among other and infinitely more valuable things, my diary.

This pattern of events was repeated three years later. Again an interesting but rather exacting *tranche de guerre*; again a painstaking effort to record, under difficulties, its essentials. We reached a wide river. We had to swim across it in the darkness. There were sixteen of us. One had a rubber tobacco-pouch. I asked him to put my notebook in it. He did; and he alone of the party failed to reach the other side. Although I dislike excuses, I now regard myself as being exempt from a diarist's responsibilities.

I suspect that diary-keeping, after enjoying for several fairly obvious reasons a renaissance during the war, is once more on the decline. The commonest excuse for not keeping a diary is that one simply hasn't got the time;

yet is one all that much busier than Goebbels was, or Ciano, or any of the other villains and mountebanks in the camp of our late enemies who left so voluminous a record of their follies for the edification of posterity? Laziness is surely a truer and more basic reason— laziness coupled, perhaps, with a sense of the outward sameness of our lives.

Many people are individualists, but comparatively few lead individualistic lives. As the conveyor-belt of routine carries us smoothly towards oblivion, what is there to record, and what temptation to record it?

It is true that prisoners, and especially prisoners in solitary confinement, have often kept interesting and moving diaries, but these recorded thoughts and emotions rather than external events, of which there were few to relieve the loneliness and monotony of their lives. Many men and women today are prisoners in a sense— prisoners of the 8.15, prisoners (while in it) of *The Times* or the *Daily Mirror*, prisoners of the office or the factory, prisoners of television. But these are prisons without bars and their inmates' sentences are self-imposed; so they are only fleetingly, if at all, aware of captivity and not at all aware—like a man in a cell—of singularity, of undergoing a strange and unnatural experience.

Besides, there are so many of them, all doing the same thing at the same time. "Train 7 minutes late" or "Train punctual for once"—is there any point in *everybody* on the 8.15 noting such facts in his or her diary? When they disperse to their different places of business, any incentive to jot down the more memorable events of the day is lessened by the knowledge that most of them are recorded anyhow on the files. "Dictated restrained memo. to J.K. on growing prevalence of pin-ups in canteen used by lower grades of staff." Why waste time writing this down in longhand when a copy of the document itself is available in a neat folder marked "Miscellaneous (Inter-Office)"?

There is, in short, every excuse for the white-collar worker not keeping a diary. Even the traveller may reasonably query the value of *carnets de voyage* full of entries like "Took off London Airport 8.15. Flew above clouds so not much to see. Landed Timbuctoo 2.45. Delayed till 4.30 by mechanical fault, but passengers not allowed out of lounge. Given coffee and biscuits. Dark soon after take-off from Timbuctoo. Captain's name is Prendergast. . . ." This sort of thing is scarcely in the tradition of Marco Polo, or even of Miss Rosita Forbes.

But of course the fact of the matter is that the best diaries always have been, and always will be, about people. Some people, and some lives, appear to be, and perhaps in truth are, duller than others; and if everybody on the 8.15 conscientiously kept a diary it is a sad fact both that the great majority of them would be quite unreadable, and that few of the diarists would—in their hearts—believe that this was so. But it is also a fact that nobody—absolutely nobody—can say for certain that if they kept a diary it might not one day prove to be a document of great interest and even fascination.

I therefore urge you (as I urged the small invalid) to carry on with your good work; it cannot possibly do any harm. The worst that anybody can say about your diary is that, "historically of small importance, it also lacks human interest," which was what a reviewer said about John Evelyn's diary in last week's *Spectator*. If immortality can be purchased with such small change, it is surely worth making a bid for it.

THE SINGLETON

I LISTENED the other day to two men arguing about giants. One was an old man, and he maintained that the reason why, when we look about us, we see no giants is because giants are recognisable as such only to the young. As we advance in years we acquire a sense of perspective. We may admire or respect an outstanding figure in this walk of life or in that, but we do not take him for a giant, since we have learnt that giants—like unicorns and Father Christmas—exist only in legends to entertain and edify the young.

To this the younger man retorted stoutly that it was no good begging the question; the plain fact was that there used to be quite a lot of giants, who were regarded as giants by young and old alike, and now there were almost none. You could not (he suggested) maintain that there was no such thing as a giant unless you also maintained that there was no such thing as Sir Winston Churchill. If one giant could exist, why could not others?

His companion took refuge in digression.

I feel myself that the younger man was right, and I would like to know what has become of the giants. It is idle to pretend that there is not a difference in stature between Hutton and W. G. Grace, between Sir Laurence Olivier and Sir Henry Irving, between Field-Marshal Lord Montgomery and Field-Marshal Lord Roberts, between Mr. Selwyn Lloyd and Palmerston. The four former may be better men over their own lines of country than the four latter were. But they are not bigger men; they are smaller men.

Wherever you look—towards literature, the law, the Church, teaching, diplomacy, golf, pugilism, or art—you get the same impression: a number of imposing and well-proportioned figures, but no giants. Why?

Different people, I find, return different answers to this question. One school of thought holds that it is all to do with beards and whiskers, and it is quite true that on the whole people *look* less portentous than they used to. If one judges purely by externals, Mr. Gladstone is bound to appear a more considerable figure than Sir Anthony Eden; but I doubt if externals really come into it very much, and in this particular case it can hardly be said that they seriously distort our perspective.

Perhaps publicity, whose aim is to project enlarged and multiple images of the individual, is in fact a less giganto-ferous medium than might have been expected, and has the same ultimate effect on reputations as an overdose of fertiliser on corn. It is true that publicity is apt to defeat its own ends, and that in many cases we should be more deeply impressed by public figures if we were confronted with them less frequently in the papers and on the newsreels.

In this connection I would say that television is inimical to gianthood. Fond as I am of Mr. Gilbert Harding, I suspect that his true status is a freak's rather than a giant's; and, in general, television, although it can make people almost infinitely famous, seems to make them at the same time rather small.

It could be argued that giants have disappeared because there is no place for them in what has revoltingly been called the Century of the Common Man; and if giants owed part of their stature to unapproachability, to behaving like Lord Curzon, there would be no need to wonder why they have become virtually extinct. But I do not think that aloofness is an essential attribute of gianthood, though it may—like a beard—be a useful accessory. Nor do I believe that the Common Man (if this dreary biped exists) disapproves of giants, still less that he somehow, subconsciously, sabotages their development.

It may, of course, be that the next batch of giants will be scientific giants, and that it is merely because oafs like me do not understand about science that we are unaware of the young entry, crouched even now over their steaming crucibles, waiting only for one or two calculations to be rechecked before they astound mankind. This would be a logical and congruous development; but there is something vaguely academic about scientific giants, and it would be nice to have some of the ordinary kind as well, like Doctor Johnson or Wellington or Nansen.

How, incidentally, does one define a giant? Not by the size of his deeds alone, for men can do great things, and even be great men, without being giants. Mr. Nehru, for instance, is not a giant, whereas I imagine Gandhi was. Stalin was a giant; Mr. Khrushchev is not. Livingstone was, Stanley wasn't. Wavell, yes; Rommel, no. . . . Although I find it impossible to demarcate the irregular frontier which separates gianthood from eminence, I seldom seem to have any difficulty in deciding who belongs on which side of it.

But all this gets us no nearer to the reason why giants have almost disappeared in these islands. In theory there ought to be more of them than there used to be. Better health, better (or anyhow more) education, more security, more leisure—all these amenities ought to be improving the breed, raising the standard of character, ability and wisdom, and thus throwing up more giants. Why are things not working out in this way?

We must, of course, have lost a good many potential giants in the last two wars; but wars are giant-makers as well as giant-killers, and I do not believe that the whole

37

explanation is to be found in the casualty lists. Perhaps we are merely going through a bad patch, and are better off than various other generations, who didn't have even a single giant to their name. Or are we, in fact, getting gradually dimmer, declining gently into mediocrity as colleges and regiments sometimes do, and as other Empires have before us?

I do not know the answer. Perhaps to ask the question is a symptom of senility; perhaps the islands teem, or at least are dotted with, giants whom younger men than I have no difficulty in recognising. But I somehow doubt whether this is the case. There may be a lot of people who think of themselves as giants, but is there more than one who has the right to do so?

THE ACTOR'S DOG

ACCORDING to my local paper, a man appeared before the magistrates last week and applied for the restoration of his driving licence; it had been suspended for a year, of which some nine months were up. "The applicant told the court he was an actor and had started rehearsals for a play shortly to go on tour. Another reason—it sounded a silly one—why he wanted a car was because this would enable him to take his dog on tour with him, which would not be possible if he had no car." His application was granted.

One of my troubles is that I seem to be able to read the newspapers in a reasonably alert and conscientious way without my eyes ever actually conveying any message to my brain. They travel down column after column of news and comment about things that matter with the same diligence with which they watch me shaving in the mirror. Afterwards I remember reading a long article about inflation, or the politics of France, in the same way that I remember having shaved; but there is precious little to choose between the intellectual increment from either process.

It is only upon matters of the utmost unimportance that my attention seems capable of riveting itself, and to these I devote the anxious thought which better men reserve for the hydrogen bomb and the cost of living index. This regrettable tendency was instantaneously brought into play by the report which I have quoted above.

My sympathies ranged themselves automatically on the side of the young actor. His admission that his wish to take his dog with him on tour might sound silly to the Olympian bench struck me as disarming; and I quite saw his point that he could not take the dog unless he had his car to take it in. Ordinary railway tickets are expensive enough, but at least some attempt is made to provide suitable accommodation for the passenger who buys one. Dog tickets are also extremely expensive, but no attempt is made to cater for the comfort of the dog or to define his rights (if any) as a traveller.

He is not, according to the regulations, allowed on the seat. If he is a large dog and the carriage is full, there is not enough room for him on the floor, which in winter is often both wet and draughty. He can be put on a chain and tied up in the inhospitable guard's van, but all dogs dislike this form of solitary confinement in noisy and unfamiliar surroundings and some dogs dislike it very much. On a long journey the dog is not allowed in the restaurant car, and although the staff are invariably ready to provide a meal of scraps or a drink of water they are not equipped with a receptacle for the dog to eat or drink out of, and the dog's master has to lurch to and fro along the corridor with an over-flowing soup-plate. And what is supposed to happen to the dog while his master has his meal?

I am an anti-guard's-van man, because I know that my dog, although he would behave sensibly, would be worried and unhappy at being separated from me. For this reason, on the rare occasions when I go to Scotland by train, I do not book a sleeper in advance but present myself to the sleeping car attendant on the train and ask whether there is an empty sleeper and if so will he connive at my dog travelling in it with me? Since this is against the regulations everything depends on the attendant; and, if he refuses, the dog and I spend the night in an ordinary compartment. This prevents us from worrying about each other and me from lying awake and composing an exigent and unreasonable letter to *The Times*. But it is not—considering how much the railways charge for dog tickets—an altogether satisfactory arrangement, and I don't see why there shouldn't be some recognised system—such as the payment of a deposit to be forfeited if the dog misbehaves itself—which would offer an alternative to the lonely austerities of the guard's van.

Glad though I am that the actor is not to be deprived of the society of his dog, I cannot help wondering how far the sagacious creature is destined to accompany him up the rungs of the theatrical ladder. Irving, it is true, had a succession of dogs. The most celebrated of them—Fussy, a terrier who had been given to Ellen Terry by Fred Archer, the jockey, and passed on by her to Irving—met his death by falling through a trap door in the stage of a Manchester theatre; next day Irving took Fussy up to London (a ticket, alas, was no longer necessary) and buried him in the dogs' cemetery in Hyde Park.

But Irving moved on a loftier plane, and in a more

feudal atmosphere, than is likely to be the case with a young actor setting out on tour today. Will his land-ladies, or the colleagues with whom—unless the play has an abnormally small cast—he will have to share a dress-ing room, take a favourable view of the dog? Much depends on the animal itself; but even if it has the nicest possible nature and is extremely well trained I have an uneasy suspicion that it may not advance the pro-fessional prospects of its owner. It may never get the chance to follow him effusively on to the stage and spoil his or (more probably and much worse) somebody else's big scene; but between them they will be lucky if, in their journey through the provinces, a tendency does not arise for the actor's fellow-artistes to refer to the dog as "that damned dog."

I hope they are lucky, all the same.

ANNUAL FIXTURE

My dear Henry,

It is very kind of you to ask me to play cricket for you against your village on August Bank Holiday. I note that you have decided to make this match an annual fixture, and before giving you my answer I will, if I may, offer some remarks on the long-term implications of your decision.

You are, I think, some ten years younger than I am, and it is just ten years since I adopted the course on which you are now embarking. I see that you have already committed one but not both of the mistakes which I made in selecting a date for the match. A Bank Holiday has much to recommend it on paper, for you can have an all-day match instead of starting after luncheon. But I assume that some of your team will be coming to

41

the game by road, perhaps from considerable distances. When making their plans these will forget, until the last moment, what driving on a bank holiday is like; they will arrive late, with frayed nerves, and their journey home after the match will be perilous and slow.

If you must play on a bank holiday, however, August is a better choice than Whitsun, when I annually challenge The Village. I take it that your scratch team will be largely selected from among your friends. Some of them will be your neighbours, some not; but very few—and fewer still as the years roll by—will have had any truck with King Willow for seven or eight months. Unlike their opponents, they will not be in practice; the broken laces in their cricket-boots will not have been replaced; and their Führer will not have had the opportunity, which generally presents itself in the course of the summer, of stiffening their ranks with some youthful demon-player seen performing in a similar match elsewhere. You were wise to settle for August.

It occurs to me (I know you will forgive me if I am wrong) that you may possibly not realise what the form is in village cricket today. A generation ago village cricket was a favourite theme for humorists, and perhaps the legend still survives that the village team is made up of rude mechanicals (with a comic vicar thrown in for good measure) whose mastery of our national game is on a level with the acting ability of Bottom, Snug and Quince. This legend is misleading. Today The Village are always formidable. I issue this warning because I remember, soon after the last war, playing for someone who, like you, was taking on The Village for the first time. "Now I don't want any nonsense," this chap told us, after winning the toss and electing to bat. "What The Village needs is self-confidence. I don't mind how *fast* you score, but don't stay there too *long*. That's what gets these fellows down." Half an hour later we were all out for 14.

But perhaps you already play, or sometimes play, for The Village? In that case you know the form, and your local knowledge will be of inestimable value to your team on bank holiday. At first your fast bowler may cavil when, while Snug is taking guard, you transfer one of his three slips to deep mid-wicket; but if Snug is in form he will soon see the point. To connoisseurs of this minor English folkway (and that is what these annual fixtures really are) there is no prettier sight than the brief colloquy between the captain of the Scratch and his bowler as The Village's No. 6 leaves the pavilion. "Isn't this the chap . . . ?" the bowler is saying. The captain nods, and the field, which had been set for Quince, is rearranged for Snug.

But this brings me, my dear Henry, to an important matter which will scarcely as yet have crossed your mind. You are embarking, not only on a minor folkway, but on a curious experiment with time. Half the point of these occasions is continuity. Your team, like mine and everybody else's, will be built around a hard core of agreeable companions, whose average cricketing ability is perhaps best described as "useful." This Old Guard, who will be drawn mainly from among your contemporaries, will be supplemented (if you are wise) by what may be called hired assassins, in the shape of undergraduates, subalterns from your local regimental depot, and other auxiliaries whose prowess as cricketers is known, or anyhow widely believed, to be above the average. But these hired assassins are a floating population, here this year, gone the next. It is the Old Guard who will form the backbone of your team down the years.

But of course the trouble about the Old Guard is that they get older. If you, Henry, could look ten years forward, as I am able to look ten years back, you would see that the passage of a decade does not improve the utility of even the most useful cricketer who was nearly forty when the decade began. Some last better than others; but you would see what I mean if, by some magical process, you could hear the applause from the other fieldsmen when one of your side holds a catch on August Bank Holiday, 1968. It will have an ecstatic, surprised, slightly incredulous sound, very different from this year's perfunctory, pseudo-professional clapping.

I don't want you to let any of this *worry* you, Henry. I only want you to understand the long-term nature of the pleasant enterprise to which you are committed. Every year the Old Guard will contribute more and more to everybody's enjoyment of the match, and less and less to your chances of beating The Village—an object which, as time goes on, you will become increasingly anxious to achieve.

I see from your letter that you have got Mark playing for you, and I agree that he will make a useful opening bowler. But he is becoming rather stout. Will he, do you think, open the bowling five years hence? And in 1968 which will be the stronger—your desire not to hurt a founder-member's feelings, or your fear that if you give Mark a couple of overs (and you can hardly give him less) The Village's tail will suddenly wag and you will present them with a bonus of 30 or 40 runs which you cannot possibly afford to give away? I should be failing in my duty as a friend if I did not warn you of the sort of dilemmas which you will have, as time rolls on, to face.

Finally, I must point out that you have already made one quite serious mistake which you could easily have avoided; you have asked me to play. I was fifty last week, and you know that I was never even a useful cricketer. Assuming that you do the correct thing and put yourself in last, I shall bat at No. 10. It is virtually certain that I shall make nought, and more than possible that I shall run you out. But it will be—otherwise—an enjoyable occasion, and we are old friends. It will be difficult for you, when we are all having drinks on the lawn afterwards, to exclude me when you adjure the company, "You must all come and play for me next year"; but next summer, when you start sending out the invitations, you will wish that you could think of some excuse for not sending one to me. If you do send one, and I accept, I shall be an established member of the Old Guard, almost impossible to superannuate yet a dead loss as far as beating The Village is concerned.

So if you have taken my point, my dear Henry, you will forgive me for writing such a long letter and thank me for refusing, at the end of it, your very kind invitation.

Yours ever,
STRIX.

THE APE AND THE QUICKSILVER

I DO not understand about finance, and I never shall. You have only got to see me paying a taxi-driver to divine that there must be something amiss in my relations with Mammon. I seem to have no effective control over the coins in my hand; I give the impression of some great, well-meaning ape who holds quicksilver in the palm of one paw and is trying to pick it out with the other paw. There is (let us say) six shillings on the clock. My intention is to give the driver seven shillings. I rarely achieve it. I become confused by the sixpences and shillings and florins and half-crowns slithering about among the pennies and threepenny bits, like *petits bourgeois* trying to hide behind proletarians during a purge.

"Sorry to have taken so long," I say at length, handing the driver either five and ninepence or eight shillings. Whether I have underpaid or overpaid him, the fact that I did not mean to do so and did not realise that I had is beyond his comprehension.

Except that I invariably give alms to street-musicians —provided I see them in time and can go through the (for me) rather tricky business of selecting a coin while on the march, without having to halt and make the deed conspicuous—all my habits in monetary matters are bad. When my children first asked me to help them divide (say) £2 9s. 6d. by 4s. 1d., I used to pretend that I was too busy, but I have since been forced to admit that their suspicions are right, and that I am no longer intellectually capable of such tasks. When I make out a cheque for £5, I write on it "Five pounds" and never "Five pounds only," which seems to me a rude and distrustful thing to do. God knows how many times cunning forgers have mulcted me of nineteen and elevenpence.

When endorsing cheques to which I am instructed, for inscrutable reasons, to affix a twopenny stamp when the sum involved exceeds £2, I do no such thing. Years ago a cheque bearing these instructions was forwarded to me in Manchuria, a land where, though it is rich in other resources, no twopenny stamps are to be had; and I carried the cheque about the Far East for more than the six months within which, I believe, the banks require cheques to be presented. I think I got the money in the end, but I resolved never again to expose myself to the risk of having to freeze funds, if that is the right expression, for lack of a twopenny stamp. Since then these stamps have been affixed, if at all, by my bank.

If individuals differ, as they certainly do, in their apti-

46

tude for finance, may not nations also differ? I have a theory that the wasting sickness which grips the British economy, and which appears to be quite incurable, is basically due to the fact that the British are very bad at dealing with money but think they are very good, thus making matters worse.

I tried this theory out after dinner the other night on a pillar of the merchant banking world who really understands about convertibility, soft currencies, the sterling area and all the rest of the mumbo-jumbo, to whom the price-structure is a mechanism no more complex than a shooting-stick, and who possesses, in addition, wisdom.

The idea was novel to him and he did not seem to think much of it. The politicians, he explained, had committed us to spending more on the Welfare State and on armaments than our war-ravaged economy could stand; therefore taxes had to be so high, and for ideological reasons to be so graduated as to penalise success, that there was small incentive to make money. The Bank of England was weak, the Treasury clueless and the trade unions strong; hence the adverse trade balance, the rising cost of living, the dwindling gold reserves and the rest of the vicious spiral. It was as simple as that.

I said I was trying to suggest that it was even simpler: that we just were not, as a nation, good enough at running our financial affairs.

"We are," I said, "supposed to be a resourceful and fundamentally reliable race. The war ended more than a decade ago. We were in a hole then; we seem to be in the same hole now, and although there may be light at the end of the tunnel no one even claims to descry it. You talk" (I said, though he had only mentioned it briefly) "of the Groundnuts Scheme. Why not bring in the South Sea Bubble, or for that matter the Black Death?"

"You say that this Chancellor of the Exchequer was an

ass, that that one was a visionary and that a third failed to rise to the occasion. You may be right. If you were explaining to me the dilemma of some Central American republic, reft by dissension between two powerful factions with wholly incompatible views on what needed to be done for the general good, I should listen to your diagnosis with respect and should refrain from investing my money, if I had any, in the municipal tramways serving the capital of so ill-circumstanced a State. But we are speaking of Great Britain, are we not?"

"*I* was," said my friend, rather drowsily.

"Our country," I remorselessly continued, "suffered grave injury in the last war. But she was not conquered. Her principal cities, though damaged, were not reduced to rubble; her factories were not blown up; half her territories were not sequestered to the control of Soviet Russia; she was not occupied by garrisons for whose up-keep she had to pay; her self-confidence was not shattered, but rather the reverse."

"Germany," my friend pointed out, "has only a token defence programme."

"She may be fortunate in that respect," I admitted, "but nothing you have said explains to me why she should, starting from a long way behind scratch, be so much more fortunate in other respects than we are. It says in my newspaper that she now holds more gold and dollars than we do, that she sells more cars and more ships and is in every way richer than the United Kingdom. No doubt she has deserved to do so well. But how have we deserved to do so badly? Can you—taking into account all the perquisites of a conqueror, all the assets represented by our national character, all the advantages derived from our Empire and all the benefits bestowed on us by the kindly Americans—can you seriously contend that our economic failure is not due to some

48

inherent and unsuspected incapacity in matters of finance?"

But my friend, worn out by a long day in the City, had fallen asleep.

THERE'LL ALWAYS BE AN ER-LAND

THE envelope bulged but was not at all heavy. What *could* it be that the British Broadcasting Corporation was sending me? White feathers? A rosette? A lock of Mr. Godfrey Winn's hair? Mystified, I opened the envelope.

Inside it, coiled up together like hibernating adders, were a dozen strips of recording tape with an average length of perhaps eighteen inches. A friendly letter from the Talks Department explained that they had been excised from my contributions to a recorded discussion programme over which I had presided as chairman. "You are apt to speak rather slowly," wrote the Talks Department. "Here, by way of gentle reproof, are some of your 'ers' which we thought it best to cut out."

If I had the skill and the equipment, I suppose I could join all these little brown ribands together and play them over to myself on a machine. It would be good for me to hear myself saying "Er . . . er . . . er . . . er . . ." over and over again for a minute or two minutes or whatever these drab noises add up to. It would teach me a lesson.

But would I benefit from that lesson? Would my speech become more fluent, more incisive, less constipated? Somehow I doubt it. I am too old to slough off what seems—I comfort myself by believing—to be a national idiosyncrasy. When my brothers and I were very young, our mother strove to break us of the habit of saying "sort of": as in the phrases "*It's sort of difficult to explain*," "*We sort of got lost*," "*He sort of fell over*." We ought, she rightly insisted, to decide what we meant to say and then say it; to blur our meaning with "sort of" was superfluous and slovenly, and for a long time, whenever she heard the expression fall from her little darlings' lips, our mother called us to order by uttering a codeword. It was (though why it was I have forgotten) "Tishbite."

We were then at a formative age, but I am afraid that the remedy did not work. I certainly, and to the best of my belief the others too, following a usage which is very general among our compatriots, still insipidly garnish our conversation with "sort of" as landladies garnish apple-pie with custard.

How is it that, when we put our hand in our pocket to dispense the bright matchless currency of our language, we bring out such a disproportionate sediment of fluff? Why, if asked a question, do we practically always begin our answer by saying, "Well"? Why, apart from the constant interpolation of "sort of," are we so loath to use an adjective without putting "rather" or "quite" in front of it or tacking "-ish" on to the end? Whence comes our insensate addiction to almost meaningless phrases like "on the whole" and "by and large"? Why do we all, all the time, say "er"?

Supposing you asked a thousand, or if you like a million, adult Britons to express *viva voce* their opinion of some non-controversial measure—say a reduction in the Entertainment Duty—of which they might all be expected to approve, in which of the two following ways do you suppose the majority would express their approval:

(*a*) "I think it is a good scheme";
(*b*) "Well, er, I think it's rather a good sort of scheme, on the whole"?

I have no doubt myself that the longer of these two formulæ would show, particularly in the South of England, a great preponderance over the shorter.

It surprises me that no inquiry has been made—either by some learned booby or by a Government-appointed working party or commission—into the loss of productivity caused by "er." It must, when you come to think of it, run into astronomical figures. Take education alone. What proportion of the school year is devoured by "er"? If all the teachers and all the pupils stopped saying "er," I estimate that between 10 and 20 per cent. more learning could be imparted in the course of a term.

Think, too, of its effect on commerce and industry, and perhaps above all on the civil service. Ask any stenographer, or any secretary who has to keep the minutes of a conference, how much of their working day is sterilised by "er." People are always proving, in time-and-motion studies, that vast sums of money can be saved by paring away from any organised activity the small, unnecessary exertions which slow it down, and progressive farmers who adopt these methods find that they can milk forty cows in the time it once took them to milk thirty. Yet speech—the bottle-neck through which all decisions are arrived at in a democracy—remains unpruned and overgrown, not only with circumlocutions and needless qualifications, but with small, ugly, pointless grunts. In Parliament, in the law courts, indeed almost everywhere except on the parade-ground and on the stage, the nation's business is being eroded by "er."

I am sure that I am not speaking only for myself when I say that, by and large, some sort of change in this really rather unsatisfactory state of affairs is, not to put too fine a point on it, just about overdue: if you see what I mean.

THE BATTLEFIELDS OF ETON

WHEN I was a small boy I was very clever, but I was also rather small. At Eton in those days enlistment in The Corps, as the OTC was called, was in theory on a voluntary basis, but in practice everyone was expected to join as soon as he entered the Upper School. I inevitably did this at a tender age and, being still under five foot four inches, which was the height at which you graduated from Eton jackets into tails, found myself posted to "G" Company.

The rest of The Corps (its Edwardian sobriquet, "the Dog-Potters," had long fallen into oblivion) was organised as a battalion of four companies. "G" Company, that cohort of lion-hearted pigmies, was a supernumerary sub-unit, a kind of runt trotting anxiously yet proudly along behind everybody else. We were not armed, like the main body, with Lee Enfields, but with carbines said to have been used by the cavalry in the Boer War; they were lighter and shorter than the ordinary Service rifles, which was just as well.

There was no National Service in those days; during your tour of duty in The Corps you went to camp every summer and not, as reasonably enough happens now, just once. I had to go four times. The great difference between infantry training in those days and in these was that there was no motor transport. Man or boy, you marched to the training area, fought a battle against Northland or Southland, and then marched back again, after which there was the now almost forgotten ritual of a foot inspection. I cannot remember whether "G" Company were excused camp, for I had grown out of their Lilliputian ranks by the time the summer came

52

round; but I do remember that one's earlier camps were rather tiring and that one greatly envied the gallopers.

These were boys—at no time, I think, numbering more than half a dozen—who were known to be good horsemen and who were mounted on chargers provided by Aldershot Command. Except for that key-figure, the mounted bugler who would eventually sound the "Cease Fire," they represented the only effective means of communication between the umpires. The umpires were also on horses and this led, indirectly, to a vogue for dates as a supplement to the haversack ration; for legend insisted that one of us had, with a blank cartridge as propellant and a date-stone as projectile, caught some poor charger in a tender spot and unseated the arbiter of strategy; but I never remember anyone firing a date-stone, even at a galloper, though the project was often discussed.

In those days the Eton College Officers' Training Corps (a designation since replaced by "Combined Cadet Force" which sounds more democratic) wore a distinctive uniform, different from the khaki worn by all other schools. The colour was a sort of pinkish dun, like the winter coat of a strawberry roan pony, but during my time it altered, as old uniforms wore out and were replaced by material bulk-purchased (according to rumour) from surplus First-War stocks intended for the kilts of the London Scottish, to a cross between rhubarb fool and bloater paste. Unlike other OTCs we wore shirts and ties (both of a hue vaguely in keeping with the rose-red-city-half-as-old-as-time *motif*) instead of high, constricting collars forming part of the uniform jacket. This sensible practice has been—rather tardily, if I may say so—adopted throughout the Army, the Royal Air Force and the police.

The other schools, whom we lay alongside in camp or encountered on manœuvres, maintained that we owed our sub-Ruritanian habiliments to the fact that, having once killed one of the "enemy" on a field day, we had been forbidden for ever to wear the King's uniform. None of our critics, however, claimed the macabre distinction of having provided us with our original victim, and we felt ourselves under no compulsion to rebut the charge. Had we known or even supposed it to be true we should, needless to say, have taken pride in it.

"*Dans le métier militaire, il n'y a que fumer,*" a French soldier had confided to one of my uncles in the First War; and in The Corps this philosophy found many adherents. The abundant opportunities for smoking were tactitly acknowledged as the only compensation of an arduous and uncomfortable existence—except, of course, for the rioting on the last night of camp, when it was customary to demolish the latrines, pour blank cartridges into the incinerator and let down the tents of other schools.

All these—the other schools—we regarded with a contempt which they cordially reciprocated. With us it was a point of honour to treat everything to do with camp as an obscure and distasteful joke, and it seemed to us that some of these other places *tried* too hard. I remember at one camp there was a school which none of us had ever heard of, called (let us say) Cooper College. It was a small school and its total armed strength amounted to only one weak but in our view excessively martial platoon. When we heard its commanding officer give the order, "At the halt—on the left—*form*—COOPER COLLEGE!" we thought it exquisitely funny. No wonder we were loathed. Only our great numerical superiority over every other contingent saved us from reprisals.

My own military career progressed, as the years went by, steadily enough. In due course I reached the rank of Company Quartermaster Sergeant; in this capacity I carried a black stick with a silver knob on the end instead of a rifle and was responsible for the hogsheads of warm ginger beer with which the sweating troops were refreshed during truces. But although being in the LOB (or Left Out of Battle) category produced many privileges and perquisites, my ambitions were not satisfied. I aspired to be a cadet officer.

While this involved the ever-present hazard of tripping over your sword, it meant that in camp you ate in the officers' mess and shared a tent and a soldier-servant with one of your friends instead of pigging it on the floorboards with eight or nine other boys. But when my promotion to this rank became—as I judged—due, nothing happened; and it was some time before I realised why.

I was by now editor of the *Eton College Chronicle* and had taken it upon myself to write the accounts of field days which appeared in that organ from time to time. In the past these had, I think, been contributed by one of the more military-minded masters and were full of references to well-executed flanking movements, orderly withdrawals and other (in my experience) quite inconceivable events. I determined on a more realistic approach. Sentences like "Throughout the action the enemy showed that readiness to retire which is so often a feature of the tactics employed by the side fighting with its backs to lunch" began to recur; and it gradually dawned on me that they were *mal vus* by those on whom my prospects of advancement depended.

So I left the next field day to be covered by my co-editor, a gifted colleger who could be relied on to keep a reasonably straight face and put in one or two of those Greek quotations which always lend tone to the profession of arms; and a few days later I tripped, for the first but not for the last time, over my sword.

I WAS A PRISONER OF THE IMPERIALISTS

"I HAVE been telling how I was expulsed from Sofia. They said I must be telling you."

This fragment of dialogue came into my mind when I read Mr. Sefton Delmer's account of his extrusion from Egypt by Colonel Nasser's subordinates. The words are those of a Bulgarian Archimandrite reporting to the Religious Department of the Ministry of Information at the beginning of the Second World War; they are taken from *Put Out More Flags*, by Mr. Evelyn Waugh.

Mr. Delmer, summarily returned to England, reminded readers of the *Daily Express* of the other countries, all at the time oppressed by some form of dictatorship, from which he has been expelled. The list, like its compiler, was impressive; and, knowing Mr. Delmer slightly, I did not for a moment suppose that his refusal to "write [as he put it] for a visa" was due to some inner compulsion to *épater les tyrans*. He was sent out for the same reason that he was sent in—because he has a talent for reporting pungently the truth as he sees it. I salute his record as an expellee.

I am the sort of person to whom things happen, if they happen at all, the wrong way round. Not only have I never been expelled from anywhere, but the only time I got into the sort of fix which has been endemic in Mr. Delmer's career the whole crux of the trouble was that the local authorities, though insistent that I had no right to be in their territory, were equally clear that they had no power to send me out of it. I implored them, again and again, to expel me; they said that it was quite

56

impossible. To make matters (as I see it) worse, all this happened, not in some terror-ridden State behind the Iron Curtain, but in a tropical holiday resort belonging to the United States of America.

The islands of St. Thomas, St. John and St. Croix, together with their satellite cays, cover an area of about 150 square miles; they were bought by America from Denmark in 1917 for $25,000,000, and are known as the Virgin Islands of the United States. (The rest of the Virgin Islands—including Dead Man's Chest, which is un-inhabited—belong to us, or rather to the Queen.) This curious archipelago is a sort of halfway house between the Greater and the Lesser Antilles, and when, a few years ago, I landed on the airfield at St. Thomas, I was on the last stage of a journey through the latter islands.

Somewhere along my complicated route I had missed a connection, so I knew, or thought I knew, that I could spend only twenty-four hours in the American Virgin Islands before catching the next plane for Puerto Rico, whence I was booked to fly to the Dutch island of Curaçao. For various reasons it was essential for me to reach Curaçao on the appointed date.

Charlotte Amalie, the capital of St. Thomas, looked an inviting place as we circled over it, a brightly painted little town clambering up the steep slopes of a scrub-covered ridge, from the crest of which the ruins of Black-beard's Castle surveyed the busy harbour. Blackbeard's Castle is alleged, on slender evidence, to have been the lair of the pirate Teach. I looked forward to an instructive day in this rather bogus place, which can be roughly described by saying that it is to the Caribbean what Broadway is to the Cotswolds.

The day was certainly instructive, but I saw very little of Charlotte Amalie. Two negro officials at the airport detected a flaw in my American transit visa and I was driven (on the left of the road: a local deviation from the American way of life) to the headquarters of the Immigration and Naturalisation Service. These were housed in a dreary office and presided over by a sad, conscientious white man called Mr. Beers.

Mr. Beers examined my passport and said in a shocked way that I had no business to be on United States territory. I pointed out that my visa had been issued by the American Embassy in London, had been accepted as valid by the immigration authorities in New York, and had been vetted by an American airline before they issued me with a ticket to St. Thomas. Mr. Beers was unimpressed. The visa was out of order and gave me no right to be there.

I said, Never mind; I was booked out on the plane next day, so he would soon be rid of me.

Mr. Beers sorrowfully shook his head. Two wrongs, he pointed out, do not make a right. Since I had no authority to come, I had no authority to go. I should have to stay on St. Thomas until the whole matter had been cleared up with Washington. He reached for the telephone and made the first of many unavailing attempts to ring up the Federal Bureau of Investigation in Philadelphia.

All day long, humbly and deferentially, I wrestled with Mr. Beers's unreceptive mind; never has a journalist striven harder to get himself expelled from anywhere. Though I watched him as a mouse watches a cat, I never divined what processes in that great slow brain finally decided him to seek a compromise; but at last he found a formula which gave me a temporary reprieve. He fished out the US Department of Justice's Form I-259, headed *Notice to Deliver, Detain on Board or Remove Aliens*, and said that he would "parole me in transit."

In fact the effect of this manœuvre was only to pass the buck, for the next stage of my journey would place me once more at the mercy of American officialdom in Puerto Rico; but he gave me a long and quite sympathetic letter to his opposite number there. This described my status as "being on shore leave under detention, if there is such a thing" and added, rather decently, "the traveller is not too much at fault and I do not believe he is the kind of traveller that it was intended to follow the general procedure on."

Overjoyed, I skipped out into the tourist-infested street, found an ex-Marine pilot with a single-engined amphibian and spent an hour or two flying over the strange congeries of islands which Columbus in 1493 named the Eleven Thousand Virgins. There were a lot of pelicans on Dead Man's Chest, and at a beach on one of the American islets we landed, tethered the aircraft to a palm-tree, and had a swim.

Next day, filled with misgivings, I found myself in an imposing office in the heart of San Juan, the capital of Puerto Rico, a populous but unendearing city. There was a sort of counter with a grille on it, like a bank, and on the far side of this a posse of lynx-eyed men, wearing uniform and what looked like sheriffs' badges, were scrutinising my passport. Like Mr. Beers, they seemed puzzled and put out. If only (I thought), if *only* they will expel me. . . .

Finally one of them came over and slapped my passport down on the counter. "There's nothing wrong with your visa, sir," he said. "It's all in order. Can't think what they were playing at in St. Thomas."

Did I demand a written apology? Did I threaten to expose in a series of trenchant articles the high-handed incompetence of the American authorities in the Caribbean?

I did not. "Oh, thank you *so* much," I said. "I'm sorry to have been such a nuisance." And I snatched up my passport and fled.

DO IT IN A DAY

I THINK it was in *King Solomon's Mines* that, when some massive shutter of rock was lowered to bar a secret passage, the witch Gagool perished beneath it "with a sickening crunch." The phrase—at one time regarded by me as the most masterly and luminous in English literature—came into my mind when at 6.30 a.m. on Sunday I closed the boot of my car. I closed it with difficulty on a sort of aspic of gumboots, mackintoshes, cartridge-bags, grouse, venison, wet clothes still warm from the drying-room and other debris, beneath which were buried the uncompromising outlines of the luggage proper. There was a sort of squidgy finality about the noise it made which reminded me of Gagool.

The inside of the car was also fairly full of gear. On what was left of the back seat Lucy and the Labrador, both roughly the same size, established a precarious co-existence. On the front seat the Relief Driver (who is seventeen and rather big for his age) and I played Mad Hatter and March Hare to Kate's Dormouse. It was a tight fit.

As we bumped round the head of the loch a parcel of hinds scattered from their early roadside grazing, and a little farther on, in the ancient twisted wood opposite the house, a cock capercailzie eyed us without approbation from the top of a knoll. Soon we were on the broad, swooping, empty main road, along the first few miles of which still stand the baulks of timber erected to prevent German aircraft from landing on it in 1940. Hoodie crows, in parties of two or three or four, were scavenging among the litter left where coaches or cars had stopped to admire the beauties of nature. The day, rather surprisingly, looked like being fine and we had it at this stage to ourselves.

"Daddy" (the inevitable query came), "how much farther is it?"

"Don't start asking that silly question yet," said the Relief Driver severely. "It's nearly 500 miles."

My first clear memories of the Highlands date from the 1914–18 War. In those days, as far as I can recall, nobody drove themselves up to Scotland. Forty years ago a car was like an elephant, and the chauffeur was its mahout; there was something special and almost sacred in their relationship, and the vehicle was not expected to respond, except perhaps over short distances, to the touch of a stranger's hand.

Did the cars that I first remember in the Highlands make their annual pilgrimage by road, under the expert guidance of mahouts? I seriously doubt it. The exigencies of wartime petrol rationing apart, I do not believe that the Panhard could have made it. She was built on the lines of a waggonette, and we children, as we sat in two rows facing each other with the pointers shivering against our bare knees, exchanged witticisms about her brakes, which were reputedly tied together with wire. (Although the brakes of that era must have been simple and even gawky contrivances, none of us ever tried, as a modern child would have done, to corroborate this legend.)

I think that the Panhard must have come by train, and the same goes for the T-model Ford, which we thought of as very dashing and up to date and mahout-free, and yet at the same time—because we had seen it used as a stage-property in Mack Sennett comedies—as funny and slightly vulgar. There was a bigger, more sedate car, a limousine, which may perhaps have made its progress northwards under its own steam.

But where were these pioneer vehicles housed? South of the Border, and even in the Lowlands, houses had spacious stables which could be converted into garages ("No Smoking on Pain Of Instant Dismissal"; the elephants were dangerous and unfathomable beasts). But most shooting or stalking lodges in the Highlands must have started without any effective form of shelter for the ponderous and lofty automobiles which first found their way thither. Why, while scholars wrangle over cave-drawings executed (if genuine) by a *homo sapiens* whom they cannot hope to reconstruct in the round, does no deviationist sidle off to Caledonia and return with a monograph entitled *A Study of the Development of the Domestic Garage on Sporting Estates in North Britain*? It might not be a particularly gripping monograph; but it would avert squabbles between learned men in one or two thousand years' time, and the subject, specialised though it is, is one well calculated to yield its secrets to the arts of modern sociology.

It was, as I remember, soon after the First World War ended that people started driving up to Scotland as a matter of course, and the breakfast-baskets that used to be put on the train at Crianlarich were relegated, with Christmas stockings and other pleasant totems, to the box-room of memory. But the journey was regarded as something of an undertaking and surrounded (from the children's point of view) with a certain amount of mumbo-jumbo, such as going to bed early on the night before you started and at the hotel where you stopped on the way and being required (in an odious phrase) to "take things easy" on the day after you arrived. When at the age of fifteen I obtained permission to travel north in a sidecar attached to my cousin's motor-bicycle I thought it unlikely that I should ever have a more exciting experience; and although I can remember little of the journey I dare say that my expectations were not far out.

As we fled south through the winding glens I thought of that motor-bicycle, and of the various small cars in which, becoming at last an owner-driver myself, I had rumbled doggedly along these roads. At that time there had been no question of "doing it in a day"; and even now I was not certain that the project was quite the thing with such a load of juvenile passengers.

But children have great resilience as travellers. Just as you think they have fallen into a coma, they suddenly revive and either embark on a pointless argument among themselves, or ask you a series of unanswerable questions, or sing "The Lincolnshire Poacher" very loudly in your ear, or demand to hear some ghastly programme on the radio. They delight in phenomena which madden you, such as the successive convoys of War Department vehicles, ambling nose to tail through the Midlands, which we had perilously to overtake. The facetiæ chalked by the RASC on their tailboards—"Pass Carefully. No Driver." "The Nasser Express"—made a powerful appeal, and when at last we were clear of these obstacles to progress, their angry complaints that there were no more convoys were only stilled when we met another fascinating obstruction—a *cordon sanitaire* of part-time bureaucrats who for inscrutable reasons were conducting a traffic census round Leicester.

However, everything really went very well, and for most of the last two hours the children were spellbound by a rather unsuitable BBC drama ("Daddy, why did he call her a bitch? She's not a dog, is she?"). There were 483 miles on the clock when the Relief Driver drew up outside our front door, thirteen hours after the start of the journey; and although I personally felt rather dazed I was resuscitated by the first letter which I opened from the pile on the hall table. It was from an insurance company, and it began:

Dear Sir,—As a man who is prepared to face facts, you must consider the possibility of your death before the week is out.

I was relieved to see that it had been written ten days ago.

THE EAR OF MEMORY

WE started talking about our favourite sounds and almost at once came up against the difficulty of divorcing them from their associations. The bells of a caravan, children exchanging confidences, wild geese crying as they rise to fly inland, the rustle of the curtain going up on a first night, pipes in the distance, a motor-boat starting in the darkness—we had to admit that we did not love our sounds for themselves alone, but because they were the distinctive flavour of a sort of *pâté maison* for which experience of one kind or another had supplied the basic ingredients. In the course of the discussion someone, inevitably, advanced the claims of the sea, of waves breaking gently on a beach, and my mind slid a long way back into the past.

The major in the Scots Guards completed his survey and sat down on an impressive shooting-stick.

"Now, gentlemen," he said, "can anyone tell me what Mr. Scrimshank has forgotten?"

We gazed with a blankly judicious air at the dispositions of Henry's platoon, lying in the heather with that taxidermised look peculiar to guardsmen on field training and pointing their weapons at the Basingstoke Canal in a very steadfast manner. In a way we were glad that Henry had forgotten something because he often failed, in our view unbecomingly, to conceal his thirst for military knowledge; in another way we were sorry, because we were all Grenadiers and had no wish for one of our number to be found in error by an officer of another regiment.

"Gas?" one of us ventured. "That yellow thing, I mean."

"It's here," said Henry in an aggrieved voice. "At platoon headquarters."

He pointed to a flat object about the size of a tea-tray lying in the open. An irregular bulbous splodge of yellow was painted in the middle of its khaki surface. If framed and labelled "Despair" or "Odalisques at Variance" by P. Chétif it would have made an adequate selling-plater in the world of modern art, but its true and even sterner purpose was to let us know when we were being sprayed with poisonous gas by hostile flying-machines; in this dread eventuality, we knew or anyhow believed, the yellow splodge would turn, as if by magic, into blue or it may have been brown.

"Sorry," said the ensign who had backed what we all recognised as a likely outsider. "I couldn't see it from here. There's a tree in the way."

A pause followed. The major's hand strayed towards the cigarette-case in the pocket of his service dress jacket (at Pirbright in those days battle-dress was no more than a disturbing and scarcely credible rumour); but he remembered himself in time and, adapting the gesture, looked at his wristwatch.

"I don't like the way he's sited his anti-tank rifle, Sir," somebody said rather desperately. He pointed to

E

the weapon, or rather to a wooden model of it; it was widely believed that we should get a real one on mobilisation, if not before. The anti-tank rifle (called, we hoped after its inventor, Boys) was a sort of elephant gun with a long, slim, stylish barrel, quite capable of stopping a taxi at a hundred yards but not really much use against tanks.

"I dare say not," said the major, "but he hasn't *forgotten* to site it. I want you to tell me something he's forgotten to do."

He looked at his watch again. The performance of military duties after luncheon induced in him, as in many regular officers in the summer of 1939, a sense of maladjustment and disorientation. He rose, shutting the shooting-stick with an incisive snap.

"Mr. Scrimshank," he said, "*you've forgotten to post an air sentry.*"

Henry looked crestfallen.

"Now remember, gentlemen," the major went on, "in the next war aeroplanes are going to make a hell of a difference. A *hell* of a difference. If you go taking up positions *without* posting an air sentry, you'll be in trouble. You've *got* to have one man who's responsible for watching the sky and reporting the approach of enemy aircraft. Otherwise . . ."

He drew a lurid picture of what would happen if we neglected this precaution.

A few months later, in Norway, in Belgium and in France, we were discovering that air sentries were not nearly as indispensable as we had been told they would be. Aeroplanes did not come suddenly upon us, flitting silently and unpredictably like woodcock down a ride. They made a din which could be heard a long way off, and as the din drew nearer not one but every man in a platoon watched the sky, thus causing much time to be wasted and many needless anxieties to be entertained.

It was not until 1941, long after air sentries had been officially done away with, that I actually posted one myself. He was a very nice man called Corporal Isted and there was something peculiar about his teeth, of which Records or some other worthy branch of the General Staff kept on sending me a sort of chart or diagram, heavily annotated. "Kept on" is of course an exaggeration. I think what happened was that, possibly to lessen the risk of both diagrams of Corporal Isted's teeth falling into the enemy's hands at the same time, they sent the one of the upper jaw first, and the one of the lower jaw a few days later. They are the only official communications I remember receiving during the campaign in Greece.

This was over by the time Corporal Isted was called upon to scan the blue Ægean sky for hostile aircraft, and we were on our way to Crete. Or rather we had been on our way until the early Edwardian steam yacht in which, with a strangely assorted company, we were embarked was bombed and sunk, stranding the survivors on a small island with several wounded on our hands. A caique from Crete sportingly came to our rescue, but the Luftwaffe dominated the sea during daylight and the caique's skipper, sensibly enough, would only attempt the return journey after dark.

For various cogent reasons this meant that first the wounded and then the other passengers, who included women and children, had to be rowed out and got on board the caique in the last hour before dusk; and although by that time most of the German bombers were on their way back to base there was a fairish risk of the caique being attacked while embarkation was going on. If this risk looked like developing, it was a matter of urgency to stop, and if possible to reverse, the cumbrous traffic between the island and the caique.

And so, because on the shore that almost-loveliest of sounds, the sea breaking gently on a beach, would kill the distant drone of the Heinkels or the Dorniers, the Pirbright doctrine became once more the party line, and Corporal Isted, his long, fair, Kentish head alert against the paling azure of the sky, took station on a knoll overlooking the bay with my whistle in his hand.

We got away in the end, though I seem to remember that on the first night there was a hitch or possibly a flap and the poor stretcher cases had to be brought ashore again; but now, whenever I hear waves break caressingly upon a beach, I begin, instead of surrendering myself to their music, to worry vaguely about Corporal Isted's teeth. Perhaps these inconsequent memories illustrate, though in an extreme form, the difficulty of separating sounds from their associations.

STANISLAVSKY AT NEWPORT PAGNELL

"PROFESSOR!" I exclaimed for the fourteenth time. "How good of you to come!"

"Id iss a brivelege," replied Ronnie in a preternaturally guttural accent. He was wearing a dark-green ulster (or ulcer, according to the children) and a Germanic-looking hat.

"You got my letter?"

The fiend in human shape nodded impatiently.

"You have ze map?" he barked.

"That's super," said the Director politely. "I'll shoot now. The light's better than it was."

"And nobody is to *giggle*," said the Film Star severely.

"No, Mummy," said the little girls. They were by now drained of laughter.

"Professor!" I began once more. "How *good* of you to come!"

We got to the last shot about tea-time. The blood-stained corpses of the Professor and his female accomplice (the Film Star, in a leopard-skin coat) sprawled in the wet grass, kippering gently in the burning wreckage of their plane while the Director waited for a break in the clouds. Around them, erupting from an ornate coal-scuttle, was strewn the buried treasure which they had attempted to purloin.

It had been an exacting day. What with catching and saddling Red Knight and Isabel (for the obligatory chase), keeping the dogs out of the picture, finding the revolver, persuading the junior members of the cast that they could not give of their best as actresses while holding live grasshoppers in their hands, and solving various other problems which do not (I imagine) arise when a Cast of Thousands is deployed in California, we had done well to finish the whole film in a day; for although, according to the Director, it will run for only about seven minutes, it is packed with incident.

The Professor, who had now been spreadeagled on the ground for a quarter of an hour, uttered a low moan; and my mind went back to the last occasion, nearly thirty years ago, when Ronnie and I were in show business together.

In those days Newport Pagnell was not widely recoggised as a centre of culture; nobody spoke of it (as for all I know they do now) as the Athens of Buckinghamshire, and I cannot recall that any dramatic critics came down from London to attend the production of *Bulldog Drummond* in which Ronnie played the villain and I the hero.

Country-house cricket survives, if it does not flourish; country-house theatricals are a vanished folkway, of which this ludicrous performance must have been one of the last manifestations. The whole thing was organised—we probably used the more descriptive expression, "got up"—by some nice people with a large house near by, and in this the non-resident members of the cast stayed during the two or three days deemed necessary for rehearsals.

The hard core of the enterprise consisted of keen followers of the Whaddon Chase, and the exigencies of the hunting field had not been without their influence on some of the casting. ("Don't you think we ought to give George something to say? I believe he'll be good for a lawn meet next season, now he's got rid of that bloody keeper.") But most of the principal parts had gone to people, like Ronnie and me, with no local roots. The play was presented in a cinema.

Bulldog Drummond is not a drama in which—as for instance in *Hamlet*—the author relies extensively on subtleties of characterisation or on verbal felicities of one kind and another. What he does rely on is the stage manager. In *Hamlet* all sorts of things can go wrong backstage without the audience being mystified or even seriously disconcerted. If, where the stage direction reads [*A flourish of trumpets, and ordnance shot off within*], either nothing at all happens or the audience hear a cock-crow which really belongs to another scene, nobody minds much; the action of the play goes forward and the little contretemps is overlooked.

It is far otherwise with Sapper's masterpiece. When, for instance, Drummond shoots out the light with his revolver, it really is pretty well essential that the stage should be instantly plunged in darkness, preferably to the sound of breaking glass. Time and again, not only the suspension of disbelief but the suppression of tumultuous guffaws depends less on what the actors say or do than on what is done off-stage. Motor-horns, pistol shots,

70

screams, the simulated cry of an owl, daggers quivering in the wall—it is phenomena such as these which are the very lifeblood of a play in which the line "My God! What was that?" (not once, I think, used in *Hamlet*) punctuates the dialogue.

Although I had only once before acted in amateur theatricals (as the Lion in *Androcles and the Lion*) I was for some reason regarded as a sort of Stanislavsky at Newport Pagnell, and found myself producing as well as playing the lead. An assistant stage manager had already been put in charge of all noises off and special effects. His name was Leslie Something; he was said to be quite fearless over timber and had been given the job to make up for his disappointment at not getting a part.

A keener man you could not have wished to find; but at the dress-rehearsal Ronnie and I, laboriously conducting our battle of wits with the aid of the prompter, realised that Leslie's grasp of his duties, and particularly of the sequence in which they had to be performed, was dangerously infirm.

"My God! What was that?" Pause. "What was what?" "Er, well, didn't you hear the cry of an owl?" *Bang!*

Leslie, once he realised that he had erred, was contrite. "I'm terribly sorry," he said. "I thought this was the scene—— Oh no, of *course*; it's the next one. I hope I shall manage better tomorrow." We all hoped this.

Towards the end of Act I the heroine's drink-sodden uncle (played in this revival by Lord Pakenham, with *real* hiccoughs) shoots himself off-stage. At the sound of the shot Drummond dashes out, dashes back, and says, "My dear, you must be brave," or words to that effect. The curtain falls with Phyllis sobbing on his shoulder. This was a bit difficult to arrange in our production as the heroine was much taller than I was; but whatever size the actors may be it is scarcely possible to start playing this scene until a shot has been fired.

On the first night the heroine and I waited in vain for the pregnant detonation. After a long, embarrassed pause I bounded into the wings. Leslie was tensely poised over a bucket full of empty medicine bottles, ready to drop a ploughshare into it. I found the pistol, fired it, and rushed back to the heroine, followed by the sound of splintering glass. "My dear," I said with manly emotion, "you must be brave."

At the second performance Leslie did not miss his cue, but afterwards one or two of the unfortunate people who had been in the audience wanted to know why the heroine's uncle had taken two shots to blow his brains out. I might have given Stanislavsky the credit for this novel and arresting touch, but his was not really a name to conjure with in the Whaddon Chase country at that time. I told them to ask Leslie.

GODLESS IN LUTON

"KEEN correspondents wanted among non-Marxist atheists interested in philosophy, ethics, psychology, languages. Special interest—pure mathematics. Write in Spanish, French or English to Mr. X." An address in Luton followed.

This advertisement appears in the current issue of a magazine called *The Humanist*, which some inscrutable wellwisher sends me regularly, and a transient sadness overcame me when I read it. How shallow, how restricted, is our knowledge of our fellow-men! How difficult it is, despite the lavish clues with which he provides us, to visualise Mr. X waiting, godless in Luton, for the postman's knock! Like some wise men, and almost all fools, I rather fancy myself as a student of human nature. Piqued at my complete inability to conjure up even a nebulous vision of Mr. X, I embarked on an attempt to reconstruct him.

His wish that his correspondents should be *keen* is easy to understand and quite likely, I should think, to be gratified. "Some of the boys here," my son once wrote home from his private school, "find it difficult to think of anything to put in their letters. I tell you this because I am one of them." Any fool can see that, if one wishes to receive letters in Spanish about pure mathematics from a stranger, it is in a spirit much less languid and bemused that the writer is expected to take up his pen. One hopes for a more zestful approach.

The Humanist is devoted to the interests of Rationalism. This I take to be a superior brand of atheism, a sort of Pullman coach in the long, slow train which is carrying us all towards, and as some hope beyond, the frontiers of physical dissolution. It is natural that an advertiser in its columns should wish to be put *en rapport* with his fellow-disbelievers. But why does Mr. X stipulate that his correspondents should be *non-Marxist* atheists? There may, of course, be something *deuxième*, something rather provincial, about Marxist atheists; but unless there is a snobbish or doctrinal reason for his embargo on them, I should have expected Mr. X to welcome the cut and thrust of ideological polemics to which their letters would give him the *entrée*. Little though I know of him, this note of caution, almost of intolerance, seems out of character.

And what—now one comes to think of it—does he want these correspondents *for*? The five branches of learning in which Mr. X declares an interest have between them an enormous scope, and I find it difficult to believe that he has read everything that has been written, in Spanish, French and English, by the leading authorities in so vast a field. If he aims merely to increase his knowledge, there are less random methods of setting about it. If on the other hand he looks forward to a brisk exchange of views, to a battle of wits which will enliven the long winter evenings while snow mantles the quaint mediæval rooftops of Luton, he may court a series of disappointments; for the intellectual calibre of non-Marxist atheists, like that of Cabinet Ministers, masters of otter-hounds and other human beings, varies widely between one individual and the next.

It might, too, have been wise to be more specific about the languages he is interested in. If a red-hot agnostic in Bilbao writes him a ten-page letter about Erse or Ki-Swahili, and if Mr. X is either indifferent to these tongues or is already hock-deep in letters about Pushtu, Croatian or Fukienese, how is he to avoid acting less considerately than a non-Marxist atheist should? And how, in any case, does one correspond about a foreign language with a complete stranger?

Dear Mr. X,
    I expect you know that the French word for a water-wagtail is *une bergeronette*, but it seems possible that you are ignorant of the derivation of this enchanting polysyllable. According to Des Tripes, with whose earlier works you may conceivably be unfamiliar, the bird was once believed . . .

A keen correspondent could, one imagines, go on churning out this sort of stuff by the ream; but it must be a hit-or-miss business, since he has no means of telling whether or not X already possesses the knowledge which he seeks to impart. If X is already in the picture, the letter rather misses its point. I am bound to say that pure mathematics strike me as a better bet than languages. You cannot look the answers up in a dictionary and pretend that you knew them already; and it is a subject some of whose devotees must, if the doctrine of fair shares has any meaning, include some non-Marxist atheists.

But as I beat my head, with uncharitable curiosity, against the brick wall of Mr. X's proclaimed enthusiasms, I began to wonder what Mr. X would make of mine. If he could see me wading in a steady downpour through an enormous bog in search of the common snipe (a small, elusive and often irritating bird whose tiny carcass has no economic value, contains few calories and normally costs even the best shot two shillings' worth of cartridges by the end of the day), would he not find me at least as incomprehensible as I find him?

I think he would. I wish him luck in a quest which I now see is no more improbable than many others, and thank him for the reminder that it takes all sorts to make a world.

ATH–BOI, AND OTHER INSOLUBLE MYSTERIES

"I CAN'T bear the idea of working in an office."

I must, in my time, have uttered these words. I like to think that I did not utter them often, partly because they are plaintive and partly because my life has been haunted in only a mild and intermittent way by the bugbears they evoke. But I have frequently heard them spoken by other people, male and female, young and middle-aged, and I cannot recall a single instance in which I have withheld from the speaker my spontaneous sympathy and support. "Office life," I have always agreed, "must be hell."

Yet as a matter of fact I spend much of my own life in an office. It differs chiefly from pukka offices—I mean the sort of offices that one associates with "office life"—in being much more uncomfortable and inconvenient than any of them; and it is in the late autumn, when the evenings begin to draw in and the wind to agitate in a discreet tattoo the metal flap marked "Letters" which is the wind's main, though not its only, means of ingress into my sanctum, that a vague discontent steals over me. I think almost with envy of the white-collar class ascending daily in powerful lifts to warm, bright, functional rooms equipped with tape-recorders and calculating machines.

The muted sociable rattle of the tea-trolley outside their doors does not interrupt their telephone conversations; mine are frequently blotted out altogether by the roar of a tractor. Their privacy is not at the mercy of scrap-iron merchants and fertiliser salesmen who, failing to observe the legend "Inquiries" over a satellite office, bring in with them a great rush of gelid air. And no *proper* office harbours in its ceiling a colony of wood-worms whose patient, unremitting efforts coat all beneath with a fine integument of dust.

In all country estate offices there tends to accumulate a detritus of uninteresting curiosities: arrowheads, fossils, the skull of a stoat, bomb-splinters, great car-buncles cut from a diseased tree, a miscellany of useless *trouvailles* which it never occurs to anyone to throw away. My office is no exception to this rule. But inter-spersed among this normal class of relics are others less congruous to their surroundings. When, and for what purpose, did I bring to my place of business a single volume (ATH–BOI) of the 1875 edition of the *Encyclopædia Britannica*? It is indeed crammed with fascinating in-formation ("The strangeness of the baths of *animal*

76

substances, that have been at various times in use, is such that their employment seems scarcely credible. That baths of milk or whey might not be unpopular is not surprising, but baths of blood, in some cases of human blood, have been used; and baths of horse dung were for many ages in high favour"); but how did ATH-BOI ever get into my office, and how will it ever get out?

The same questions might be asked, with equal pertinency, about a complete set of Linguaphone records in Chinese.

The Goon-like inconsequence of this jetsam would not bring on a feeling of malaise if only the essential appointments of my office made more sense. For it must not be thought that I have surrendered to the forces of obsolescence and decay. On the contrary! Every year some modernisation is effected. I can now for instance, with the aid of an instrument which looks as if it had at one time been on tour in *Journey's End*, telephone to the estate mechanic in his workshop, provided that he has not got "Workers' Playtime" switched on too loud; and the real telephone is equipped with a wonderful bit of patent flex which never gets in a tangle and was sent me by its manufacturer after I had written a humorous article about the intransigence of ordinary telephone flex. The old grate, which used to fall apart and set fire to the threadbare carpet, has been replaced by a new one, and a large hook has been fixed to the porch outside, hitched to which my horse, if I ride to the office, gazes reproachfully at me through the window. All the time thoughtful improvements of this nature are being put in hand.

But still there is something not quite *right*, something slightly surrealist about the place. Nothing could look solider or more respectable than the glass-fronted bookcase or the nine volumes of Coates's Herd Book arrayed, with Knocker's *Digest of Workmen's Compensation Cases* and kindred tomes, upon the middle shelf. But why should the shelf below it house Darling's *Pyrometry*, six copies of a German translation of one of my books, *Who's Who* for 1920, a small empty bottle labelled "Concentrated Orange Juice," a large full bottle labelled "Tincture of Iodine. Poison," a bundle of Christmas cards, and one Egyptian piastre? I am not a finicky person, nor one who sets much store by the Art of Gracious Living; but why do I have to have Darling's *Pyrometry* among my *lares et penates*? What *is* pyrometry, anyhow?

Then there is the problem of one of my maternal great-grandfathers, an Irish baronet and a surgeon of renown. A copy of his portrait by Millais stands on the floor behind a leather sofa. Since it is a practically life-size portrait there is no room for it on the walls, and Sir Richard's dignified, sardonic profile looms up over the back of the sofa like someone who has been persuaded, against his better judgement, to play the Gravedigger in an amateur production of *Hamlet*. When anyone sits down on the sofa a cloud of tiny white feathers flies out through the holes which the dogs have scratched in the leather; and as these settle slowly on the antiquated or irrelevant appointments of my office I often have the illusion that a look of weary disgust passes across the face of my maternal great-grandfather.

This always reminds me that one of these days I must have his head cut off and framed in a picture of manageable size. Besides being inherently disrespectful, this act has been so long postponed that the thought of it fills me with a double dose of guilt. Office life may, as I have so often opined, be hell; but it really ought not to confront one with problems of this kind.

And yet, despite all its drawbacks and follies (one

78

huge drawer has never contained anything except nine composition billiard balls and a mousetrap), I would not change my office for a proper one, with graphs on the walls, fluorescent lighting, silver photograph frames on the desk and a picture of an extensive factory over the mantelpiece. It is not commodious or up to date or within easy reach of anywhere that matters; but once, stepping out of it into the dusk, I saw a woodcock go roding through the grey air a few feet above its roof, and one can put up with a lot from an office where that sort of thing has happened, and may happen again.

PROTEUS-BLIMP

THE fall of Crete had been admitted by the BBC that morning. We were in a bad way in the Western Desert. The whole country was acutely aware of disaster.

A number of ensigns newly commissioned in the Foot Guards were attending, at Pirbright, a lecture on the traditions and conventions of the Brigade. These officers, few of whom were anything like as young as ensigns are in peace-time, had been through Caterham the previous winter. At this establishment their training as recruits—rigorous enough at the best of times—had been rendered particularly testing by the German Air Force, elements of which bombed London almost nightly while they were there. The lecturer's audience had some understanding that war was a serious business.

"And finally, gentlemen," the senior major who was giving the lecture concluded, "I want you to remember one other extremely important thing. *Never* wear pink out hunting when the Court is in mourning."

This story (which, though true, is perhaps just too far-fetched to furnish the theme of an Osbert Lancaster

79

cartoon) came into my mind when I was reading *Gallant Gentlemen: a Portrait of the British Officer*, by E. S. Turner (Michael Joseph, 18s.). It would be difficult to find a more ludicrous example of the manner in which military tradition is handed on; and yet, because the episode is so very much in character, nobody—or anyhow nobody who has ever served in the Brigade of Guards—will see it as a regrettable solecism, as a sign of the tradition's weakness. It is rather, in a curious sort of way, a symptom of the tradition's strength.

We have long been accustomed to speak of the Armed Services as professions, co-equal with the Church, the law and medicine. Mr. Turner's excellent book reminds us how inapt any such comparison is. A doctor or a lawyer or a clergyman no doubt sees, in the course of his career, certain changes in the scope and technique of his profession, and no doubt he thinks of them as big changes. But they are as nothing to the unpredictable revolutions which convulse the profession of arms during the same period. Only if half the laws were changed, half the prayer book scrapped, and half the human anatomy radically altered once every twenty years would the lawyer, the clergyman and the doctor be in the same case as the Regular officer in any of the three services. Yet it is these last, as Mr. Turner points out, who have established almost monopolistic rights in the epithet "hide-bound."

Soon after the last war Mr. Turner wrote, under another name, a book called *The Third Pip*, which was one of the funniest I have ever read about the Army. His present work is scholarly, entertaining and fair-minded. Bad officers, he observes, tend to leave ampler traces in the annals of their service than good officers; after recounting the episode of Dyer at Amritsar (and recalling that, when in a libel case five years later the

80

Judge vindicated Dyer's conduct, Ramsay Macdonald told Parliament that the court's decision would have a "bad effect on Indian opinion"), he writes: "The public which shook its head over the Amritsar headlines heard, and cared, next to nothing about those officers who, far from shedding blood, tirelessly prevented the spilling of it."

His researches, which have been notably thorough, have rescued from oblivion many fascinating scraps of information. When, for instance, the Royal Air Force came into being in 1918, "some curious titles had been proposed for the new officer ranks. One list began with ensign and lieutenant, then continued with reeve, banneret, fourth-ardian, third-ardian, second-ardian, ardian, and air-marshal. Ardian is compounded of two Gaelic words and is translatable as "Chief bird."

His judgments are shrewd. In the last war, he considers, "the piquancy had gone out of Staff-baiting, chiefly because the quality of Staff work, in nearly all theatres, was high." It *had* to be high. . . . The planning Staff Officer emerged from the war with as high a reputation as he is ever likely to acquire. And: "All colonels were by now [the middle Thirties] Blimps. If David Low had made Blimp a bishop (as he once contemplated) the gallant company of colonels would have been spared much ridicule; yet it is probable that making Blimp a colonel was a salutary thing for the Army. The ceaseless barrage of ridicule and criticism could hardly fail to induce in the more conservative military minds a mood of self-examination." It requires somebody better qualified than I am to suggest how vigorous would have been the religious revival which, on this reasoning, Mr. Low narrowly failed to bring about.

I found this a fascinating book. It could easily have been no more than a tapestry of amusing *faits divers*, strange anomalies and forgotten scandals; but **Mr.** Turner has a good understanding of the fighting man and his commanders, and in its light has produced a well-documented and discriminating study of the profession of arms as practised down the centuries by an essentially unmilitary nation.

THE MIRROR AT MONGER'S

I HAD my hair cut this morning, at Monger's in Mandrake Street. If I were a methodical person and kept a diary, today's entry might include (for very little else has happened so far) the words "Had hair cut." It is inconceivable that they would be followed by "at Monger's," since I have never, in London, had my hair cut anywhere else. It would be like writing "Overslept in bed" or "Write foolish article with pen."

One of the differences—in these islands at any rate—between men and women is that men hardly ever look at their faces. They see them, but without really seeing them, when they shave, when they brush their hair, when they tie their ties; but after a certain age a merciful negligence dominates a man's relations with his face. His features were among the cards dealt him, years ago, at the beginning of a long, slow, absorbing game. As the game goes on he realises both that they are not trumps and that he cannot discard them; and unless he is an unusually vain man he examines them in an increasingly perfunctory way.

In the distant past, when he was troubled with pimples, was first in love, or had to decide for or against growing a moustache, he subjected his face to a searching and semi-continuous scrutiny. However unpleasing or even (to others) repellent its appearance, he acquired a staunch, irrational loyalty to his face. He may have envied other youths their height or their carriage or their muscles; he may even have admitted that they were better-looking than he was. But he would not—however mistaken, in the eyes of an impartial observer or even of his closest friends, this attitude may have appeared—he would not have exchanged his face for anyone else's.

In a barber's mirror one's face acquires a certain novelty, a quality almost of surprise. It has a disembodied look. The sort of surplice beneath which the rest of one's person is concealed heightens the impression that one's face has been temporarily detached, has ceased wholly to belong to one; and this impression is reinforced when, after the shampoo, the barber waggles it about as he dries one's scalp, brushes hair down over the upper part of it, and subjects it to various other minor indignities which one's face is not used to undergoing at the hands of a comparative stranger.

On me, anyhow, the effect of this spectacle is to stimulate interest in the thing: and today, as I peered meditatively at this curious exhibit, this roundish, reddish, turnip-type object vibrating impotently under the barber's vigorous towelling, it suddenly struck me that it was forty years since, as a boy of nine, I had first had my hair cut at Monger's and that I had then quite possibly stared into the very same mirror at a much earlier version of the very same face.

Monger's was not Monger's in those days, but Mee's; and the words "Mee's in Mandrake Street," spoken by my mother to the chauffeur at Victoria Station, lay across the threshold of the holidays with a sort of pointless inevitability, like SALVE on a Victorian doormat. I cannot remember who cut our hair at our private school, but my mother had the lowest possible opinion of his craftsmanship and her first concern was to repair the ravages caused by this vandal's clippers. So we were hustled along to Mee's in Mandrake Street as though for some life-saving inoculation, and deposited there with the injunction, "*Don't* let them put any of that horrible hair-oil on." Mee's unguents were then in regular demand among the crowned heads of Europe (a market which, though unhappily contracted since those days, Monger still supplies), and I cannot believe that any of his hair-oil could truly be described as horrible; but my mother thought its application unbecoming to her small sons, and in this matter they were at one with her.

Once we forsook Mee's and went to another place. I cannot remember why this was—perhaps we failed to deter the devoted barbers from completing their ministrations and came out smelling like crowned heads—but the other place was not a success. The man who was cutting my brother's hair reproached my man with not having gone to the war. My man said he was over age, and to me he seemed incredibly senile—thirty or forty at the very least; but he began to tremble with indignation and soon buried his reeking scissors in the lobe of my ear, causing a copious flow of blood. After that we went back to Mee's where, even after whatever *coup d'état* converted it to Monger's, I cannot recall any comparable incident occurring during the last few decades.

Remembering these things, I wondered what agency or influence—apart from it merely getting older and older—had done most to turn the face which first looked into that mirror forty years ago into the object which it reflected this morning. I do not know the answer, nor would it be of general interest if I did; but I do think that a fascinating study could be made of the manifold ways in which professions and hobbies, as well as virtues and vices, help to mould people's features.

Horses and the sea are perhaps the two external influences which leave the clearest marks on faces. Horses do not do this in some mystical manner, but because when a human being imposes his or her will on a horse the effort automatically contracts the facial muscles, and particularly those round the jaw, in a certain way. You see this process at work in small children as they ride their ponies over jumps in a gymkhana; and you see the same *sort* of thing at a lower level if you look at the men employed in a cattle market to herd the beasts into the auctioneer's ring. Their faces are lined by the effort of continuously imposing their will on animals; but, because the effort calls for no tolerance or finesse and involves no serious risk of defeat, the lines produce a crude, heavy, impersonal impression, and the total effect is coarse and often brutal. In the horseman's face (at its best) the lines sketch judgment of dangers as well as audacity, understanding as well as determination.

The "typical" naval officer's face looks as if it had been weathered into its final form by watch-keeping under exposed conditions; and perhaps in a generation or two this face will disappear, as less and less time is spent scanning the sea from a wind-swept or a sun-scorched bridge, and more and more is spent scrutinising instruments in the equivalent of an office. I hope this will not happen.

You have only got to go to a dog show to see that dogs have their influence on the human face, though it is less marked and less standardised than that of horses. At the beginning of the last war I met two senior officers who were in charge of the carrier pigeons belonging respectively to the Army and the RAF; both spoke in gentle, cooing voices, raising and lowering their heads on their necks as they did so. For all I know there may be a tropical-fish-face.

But we have wandered a long way from Monger's (formerly Mee's), and perhaps you have had enough—as I had by the time the barber had finished his work—of my reflections.

ELEPHANTS AND ESSAYS

THERE are moments, and this is one of them, when I think almost wistfully of examinations. As a lad, I was very good at these horrible things. I never quite attained the devil-may-care *expertise* of Lord Pakenham. He it was (or him, anyhow, we firmly believed it to have been) who, after dashing off the whole of a Greek composition while the other candidates were still struggling with the first two lines, noticed on reading it through that by a slip of the pen he had put the subject of one sentence into the accusative. A lesser man would have corrected the error; Lord Pakenham merely added a footnote which read: "This use of the accusative is not recommended to younger students."

My success as an examinee was due to audacity of a different and much less splendid kind. I hardly ever knew the answer to any given question, but I generally knew part of it. When asked, for instance, "What do you know about the Defenestration of Prague?" the true answer was "Precious little"; such matters as the date, and who defenestrated whom, often eluded me altogether. But my ignorance acted as a spur, and the less (up to a point) I knew about a thing the easier, and indeed the more necessary, I found it to write as though I actually knew a great deal. Tushery of a semi-specious kind poured from my pen. I found that if one began, "Prague, on that momentous Tuesday, was strangely quiet for the time of year," the odds on one having made

86

a mistake in a matter of ascertainable fact were only 6—1, and it was moreover highly probable that the examiner had not the slightest idea on which day of the week the defenestration took place. It would have been silly to guess the month, with odds of 11—1 against being right, and there was no future at all in guessing the year. After "on that momentous Tuesday" the examiner could hardly expect one to furnish him with such mundane details as the actual date; and, besides, this rather Guedallan approach gave the impression that the subject had fired one's imagination. Which, in a way, it had.

The weekly essayist is on paper much better off than the examinee, yet in some ways I think I found the latter role more congenial. There were strains and risks attached to an examination, as there are to a point-to-point; but to ride over the course in your own time, without a starter or a judge, is a cold-blooded and unrewarding business and if, as sometimes happens, put off until the last minute is apt to engender a mood of remorse and self-reproach. Surely, the essayist tells himself, there are tests less exacting and better worthwhile which are within my capabilities?

It was in such a mood that I read of the death, last Monday, of Mr. Philip Fernandez, the head elephant-keeper at the Belle Vue Zoo in Manchester. He was sixty-eight, and he claimed to have walked 20,000 miles alongside elephants carrying children on their backs.

The thought of such a career filled me with envy. I am fond of walking. I like elephants; I once shot partridges from the back of one (an extraordinarily difficult thing to do) and formed a high opinion of those sagacious beasts. Compared with writing essays, conducting how-dah-loads of children round a zoo, even in Manchester, seems to me a blissful way of life.

It might become montonous after a time. I dare say

anxious mothers would be rather a bore, and sometimes, no doubt, a child would be elephant-sick; but at least the elephant would be *there* all the time, waiting to be led around, whereas the essay, though waiting to be written, is often not there at all.

People would say that one was getting into a rut; but surely a weekly essayist is in a rut already, and a rut lacking—since each essay must differ, however fractionally, from the one before—in the comforting amenity of sameness? I should find it easy to ignore such criticisms.

No; it is an almost idyllic picture that the late Mr. Fernandez has conjured up. I see myself striding proudly through the thick Manchester dusk. Beside me ambles Forsythe (or whatever the elephant is called) bearing the day's last load of happy toddlers on his back. From his vast belly, somewhere above my left ear, a faint, euphonious rumbling signals his pleasureable anticipation of the evening meal. His breath hangs like shell-bursts on the frosty air. When we return to base, he kneels and the children de-pachyderm with many feeling expressions of their gratitude to me. Then Forsythe and I repair to his lofty stable, where I give him his feed and, with the help of a step-ladder, rug him up. And so to my humble lodgings.

You ask what I shall find to do in the evenings? I have a ghastly suspicion that I may, from sheer force of habit, write essays for the *Spectator*.

TO WHOM SENT

I SUPPOSE that hardly anybody keeps a game-book nowadays. I have done so, with one or two regretted lapses, since 1918, and the other day I came across the little brown book in which I began these annals at the age of eleven.

It is called The Pocket Game Register and bears the even earlier date of 1901: an inscription on the fly-leaf shows that it was handed on to me by an aunt. Other evidence makes it clear that these pocket-books were given away free to their customers by the Schultze Gunpowder Company, whose motto—*Inter Fulmina Securus* —no doubt expressed the hope rather than the conviction of a grown-up on finding that he had the youthful Strix for a neighbour at the covert-side.

Textual evidence suggests that even in those early days my addiction to the sport had an unbalancing effect. For instance, the entry for August 16, 1918, reads: "15 rabbits, 1 BUᴢᴢARD"; in the Remarks column appears the Bunterish and surely rather non-U monosyllable, "Gloat!!". I was an intelligent and well-lettered little boy, and the emotions consequent upon shooting a buzzard with a 28-bore must have been powerful indeed to make me write its zz the wrong way round.

Seven years later my mother gave me a proper game-book, a strong leather-bound volume whose pages are free from the plugs which the sponsors of the Pocket Game Register felt justified in inserting: *Col Cody (Buffalo Bill) writes: "We have used Schultze Powder with the Wild West Show for the past five years, and it has given entire satisfaction."* . . . *In 1892 the Grand Prix du Casino, Monte Carlo, was won by Count T. Trautesmandorf, who writes: "I won all my prizes last year with Schultze Powder."* To this game-book I transferred the more memorable of my early records, and I am still using it today.

It was devised and printed by A. Webster and Co., 44 Dover Street, Piccadilly, W.1 (established 1780 at 60 Piccadilly, W.1), in an era when, clearly, bags were expected to be large and every day's shooting to be followed by a display of feudal munificence. On the left-hand pages the narrow columns headed Grouse, Pheasants, Partridges, Woodcock, Hares and so on are preceded, as usual, by wider columns headed

Date | Where Killed | No. of Guns

and are followed by a generous space for Remarks. The right-hand pages are a replica of their counterparts except that for Where Killed and No. of Guns is substituted a single capacious column above which appear the words To Whom Sent. I have to confess that in my game-book for the past thirty years these words have been scratched out and replaced by the headings on the left-hand page, thus allowing both pages to be used for the same unbountiful purpose.

You are at liberty to believe, on this evidence, that I am the sort of curmudgeon who habitually eats twelve teal at a sitting instead of dispatching two or three of them to his old governess in a basket. But this belief would not survive scrutiny of the terse but ample records which (now I come to think of it) would provide a biographer with the only solid documentary foundations on which to reconstruct my career.

These records show that my sporting activities have not followed the pattern which A. Webster and Co. had in their minds when they designed my game-book. The pages abound in entries to which the words To Whom Sent would make an inapposite sequel; for often there has been nothing to send. "Not a bad day, as blank days go" is one fatalistic comment; but many of the days on which nothing, or next to nothing, was shot were exceptionally arduous and inclement. I see that on one of them—in the Outer Hebrides in September, 1926—"the spring tide cut us off from the boat. This involved a rather cold swim, followed by a long, hard row home in the dark." The whole book is full of entries like "Torrential rain. Walked from 9.30 till 6 but only saw 3 snipe." These are not merely the follies of youth (like, for instance, such distant echoes of one's Hunt Ball days as "Shot v. moderately after the usual 2 hrs. sleep plus a 60 mile drive"); on one day last season two guns brought back from "7 hrs. solid climbing and walking in mist and rain with half a gale blowing" only three grouse and three ptarmigan. To Whom Sent, indeed!

Keeping a game-book is my only good habit. Many people, who disapprove of or despise shooting, would not regard it as a good habit at all, but as an uncultured and even barbarous aberration. Yet I persuade myself that it is at the worst a harmless thing to do. The disappointments and elations which are prosaically chronicled would make the dullest possible reading for anybody else; and even for me, because I have a bad memory, a lot of the details have faded into an almost meaningless blur. Not all the place-names in the Where Killed column still conjure up a landscape; Crockatee and the Devil's Spittoon. Uillt Fearna and Loch Middle, Stronafian and the Abingdon Sewage Farm—these and many more are no longer valid passwords to the past.

But other place-names—partly because I am still lucky enough to live on the land where I was brought up—recur again and again down the years, and with them the names of my friends, and latterly of their sons—and my son— as well. So I continue stolidly, without misgivings, to tot up the often exiguous bags and to write beside them such unevocative comments as "V. wet. Not much seen. Missed a stoat in Dead Man's Lane," sustained by the vague conviction that this unexacting life-work has some purpose.

What that purpose is I could not possibly tell you. I suppose it is merely to give myself pleasure, to stitch a kind of faded tapestry on which, when I look at it, figures of men and dogs, the outlines of woods and cliffs and lochs and mountains, reveal themselves, odd incidents and small triumphs are re-enacted, and beauty is here and there mistily apprehended.

If this is the object of the exercise, it can do nobody any harm; and although I dare say that keeping a game-book is not in truth a good habit, I do not think it is a bad one and I hope I shall never give it up.

THE TREASURE SEEKERS

As it sank towards a zareba of blackthorn hedges the January sun, intruding across Leicestershire like a distant, eccentric, but lovable relative, cast its beams upon the conference table. As it waned, the flames licking the logs in the grate lost their ineffectual pallor and, though they gave out no more heat, seemed to give out more.

The documents on the conference table derived no such benefit from the winter sunlight. The copies of old charts, the aerial photographs of the reef, the faded cur-licue script in which Spanish bureaucrats recorded a grievous loss 300 years ago, the photostat log of the English sea-captain who later made a killing at this wreck (or perhaps at another), the statistics about the rate of growth of coral—these really needed to be scruti-nised by candle-light, or in the blaze of a Caribbean noon. The well-bred lambency, slanting in through the big Georgian windows, made it easy to detect a garishness, a touch of Wardour Street, in the exhibits we were assembled to mull over. The brown ink on the old docu-ments looked *too* brown, and a light which would have brought out all the best in a muffin brought out all the worst in the coloured photographs of tropic seas and embedded anchors.

As I listened to the White Russian describing an earlier attempt upon this wreck ("the detection-gear was *com*-plitly useless") I remembered something a wise man had told me many years ago. I was seeking a title for my first book, which described an improbable and outlandish enterprise. He said: "*Treasure Island* is the best title in English literature. Every word in the title of a book ought to stake a claim on the reader's interest. Everybody has a weakness for islands, everybody is fascinated by treasure; and everybody has read *Treasure Island*. I don't believe *everybody* would have read *The Sea Cook*."

At the time I took it for granted that he was right in what he said about the allure of treasure; and in the course of a mis-spent life I have, rather surprisingly, never dabbled in putative doubloons. It was only last Sunday, not far from the spruce kennels of the Quorn, that I saw how intoxicating is the faint and slightly phoney scent which treasure leaves behind it down the centuries.

Given a number of clues pointing to the existence of treasure, I do not believe that it is humanly possible for a man to disbelieve in the treasure's existence. He may decide that the chances of finding it are nil, or that it is in some place other than that to which the clues point; but he is, or becomes, unable to reject the whole story.

It is typical of the business that on Sunday afternoon we finished up with two treasures instead of one.

The *Santa Maria*, bursting with bullion, went on the reef in 1637. For the next three years strong Spanish expeditions, ordered to salvage her cargo, failed for a variety of reasons to reach the reef. It is a long reef, but the depositions of the numerous survivors from the *Santa Maria* at a court of inquiry describe with general accuracy the scene and circumstances of the disaster.

Fifty years later Captain Snooks, searching for treasure—perhaps the *Santa Maria*'s—along the same reef, struck lucky. In a few weeks his Indian divers had made possible the recovery of thirty tons of specie, mainly silver but some gold. ("A ton of gold doesn't take up much room, you know. I should say that a *solid* ton would be about the size of that card-table. What do you think, Hugh?" "Ye-e-e-s. A bit smaller, probably." This is the sort of dialogue into which the treasure-seeker finds himself lapsing.)

Snooks cleared one "roome" and, at a slower rate, part of another, then sailed for England, renown and a knighthood. In his absence a swarm of interlopers in small craft removed further pickings from "Neptune's exchequer"; from the accounts of the British authorities, who were trying to exact the Crown's dues (a tenth of the treasure recovered) the less accessible parts of the *Santa Maria*, already overgrown by coral, did not yield much to these scavengers.

Nor did they to Snooks when he returned later in the same year. He "wanted engines," according to one account, to get through the encrusted timbers. Lightly laden, he left the scene of his triumph for a career of useful public service in the colonies. He never went back to the wreck, nor did he sponsor any further attempt upon it.

We know roughly what the Spaniards lost in 1637; we know more precisely what the British gained half a century later. If Snooks and the scavengers were working the *Santa Maria* wreck, they left many millions of pounds' worth of precious metal under its coral carapace. If—as a comparison of the Spanish and the British documents suggest—they were working another, unidentified wreck, they may have cleared her, for fifty tons of bullion was a normal load when treasure was dispersed among the better-found ships in a convoy.

But in 1637 the whole treasure was in the decrepit but capacious hull of the *Santa Maria*. The Spanish admiral objected on seamanlike grounds to her use for this purpose; but a Spanish general was in charge, and it was probably an inter-Service squabble which immured in the coral the equivalent of almost any sum you like to name on a Sunday afternoon in Leicestershire.

It may be there still; and if, after the insight I have given you into the treasure-seeker's mentality, you suppose that 1637, and the *Santa Maria*, and Captain Snooks are reliable clues, I shall be disappointed. There are no reliable clues to treasure. It would not be there if there were.

A GOLDFISH'S FAREWELL TO HIS BOWL

"It was great fun writing a book. One lived with it. It became a companion. It built an impalpable crystal sphere around one of interests and ideas. In a sense one felt like a goldfish in a bowl; but in this case the goldfish made his own bowl. This came along everywhere with me. It never got knocked about in travelling, and there was never a moment when agreeable occupation was lacking. Either the glass had to be polished, or the structure extended or contracted, or the walls required strengthening." Sir Winston Churchill, who thus recalls in *My Early Life* his sentiments when he was at work on *The River War*, goes on to compare writing a book with building a house or planning a battle or painting a picture.

It is lucky for us, and for our descendants as well, that this great craftsman has continued to find pleasure in the tasks of authorship. But to one of these tasks I find a later reference puzzling. Did Sir Winston *really* enjoy correcting the proofs of the two "massive" volumes of "my *magnum opus* (up to date) upon which I had lavished a whole year of my life"?

It seems certain that he did correct them. He had had an unhappy experience with an earlier work, *The Malakand Field Force*. Being stationed in India when he completed the MS, and anxious to avoid unnecessary delays in publication, he delegated the proof-reading to an uncle who, although "a very brilliant man," did his work so ill that the *Athenæum* called the end-product "pages of Napier punctuated by a mad printer's reader"; the ubiquitous misprints were responsible for the only note of reservation in the general acclaim.

He tells us that he did some midwifery on his second book: "All the hard work was done and I was now absorbed in the delightful occupation of playing with the proofs." It is a pleasing glimpse of the young Hussar who, after a tour of duty with the Lancers which ended at Omdurman, had embarked on his long, frequently interrupted, and partially successful masquerade as a civilian; but there comes a moment when the author must stop playing with his proofs, when the goldfish can no longer embellish the walls of his bowl, when the by now sickeningly familiar pages provide a stern and anxious duty rather than a delightful occupation. All who have lived through this hour full of petty but irrevocable decisions (in which I live now) will be glad to know that it left no scars on the youthful Churchill.

Having always a soft spot for small, inarticulate minorities, I will begin by explaining to those readers who have not yet written books themselves that the first proofs you get from the printers are known, doubtless for some good reason, as "galleys." These are elongated strips of paper upon whose surface your jewelled prose seems to go on and on and on, producing on the eye much the same lack-lustre impression as it might gain from the less interesting reaches of the Basingstoke Canal. No especial problem is involved in correcting the galleys—unless, of course, after doing so you leave them in a place where they can be torn to shreds by your Labrador puppy. Anyone who is imbecile enough to do this has to start the whole job over again on a spare set of galleys which the far-sighted publisher provides, presumably against just such a contingency.

The next thing that happens is the arrival of page-proofs. These, since they look more or less like an actual book, though without any binding, present a less dispiriting appearance than the galleys. In my case, it is at this stage that grave doubts about one's basic qualifications as a writer begin to arise.

Until I started work on the page-proofs I had, without thinking very much about it, supposed myself the master of a vocabulary which, if not rich, was at least adequately diversified. But my publisher, a man of discrimination, tactfully drew my attention to a tendency for certain words and phrases to recur throughout my narrative; and when I looked into the matter I found that my style could be said to coruscate only in the sense in which this verb can be applied to the electric advertisements in Piccadilly Circus. The effects achieved—or strained after—were highly repetitive. A rich vocabulary, indeed! In 100,000 words I seemed to have relied almost exclusively on half a dozen adjectives: bleak, swift, feckless, chimerical, *désorienté* and far-flung. A few others had crept in here and there on sufferance; but the incessant intrusions of the Old Guard produced a mannered and monotonous effect.

Further blemishes revealed themselves in every branch of usage. What streak of ingrained pomposity had made me write, again and again, "It would seem" when all I meant was "It seems"? Why did I keep on inserting, quite superfluously, "at the time" ("It was believed in London *at the time* that")? Whence my extreme reluctance to find English equivalents for foreign words like *ignis fatuus* and *coup de main*? Where did I pick up the bureaucratic infection which had caused me to write "adverse weather conditions" instead of "bad weather"? Like a djinn materialising out of a bottle, there emerged from the proofs a literary *alter ego* of a most unprepossessing kind.

Purged of their grosser solecisms, the page-proofs went back to the printer; and now I am wrestling with a revised set. This is my last chance. In a day or two the goldfish will be bereft of its bowl, and no more attempts to remedy defects in the glassware will be possible.

I enjoy playing patience, but not a patience that will never come out; to such a pastime correspond my endeavours to ensure that the illustrations (which for technical reasons can only be inserted after pages which are multiples of sixteen) appear in roughly apposite sections of the text. The 300-odd pages, each of which now bores me till I could scream, are littered with unsatisfactory compromises. This frightful book deals with the last war. How, in writing about the Germans, can one be consistent in italicising the names of their organisations?

Gestapo is surely part of the *lingua franca* of twentieth-century civilisation; to put it in italics would be as unnatural and affected as to pronounce Paris in the way the French do. Yet *Abwehr* and *Sicherheitsdienst*, which were strictly comparable organs of the Nazi State, clearly demand italics. If you write *Führer*, must you write Göring? And Göbbels? For these bleak and far-flung problems, chimerical if not actually feckless solutions will have (it would seem) to be found—and swiftly—by the *désorienté* author.

But at least in a few days a process which only an exceptionally buoyant personality could describe as "the delightful occupation of playing with the proofs" will be over: unless indeed Sealion once more gets his teeth into them, and I have to start all over again.

This, however, is not a likely contingency, the puppy's *savoir-faire* and deportment having improved since he chewed up the galleys. Even if it occurs, it can only postpone the inevitable. I suspect that I, like other gold-fish, will miss the shelter of my brittle bowl when it has gone off, ahead of me, on the path towards oblivion.

NOTES ON A VOYAGE

APPLE-CHEEKED was the word to describe the taxi-driver. Elderly, courteous, and when it came to suit-cases herculean, he seemed to belong to the imagined past, to have driven, perhaps, a troika in Strelsau.

"There she is, Sir," he said, pointing up at the bows of the liner as we turned into the large hangar alongside which she was moored. "You're in plenty of time."

The interior of the hangar closely resembled that of the Reading cattle market; but it was more spacious, and therefore colder. Its floor was subdivided by a labyrinth of movable hurdle-type steel barricades. In the centre of the corrals thus formed, solid, overcoated officials lounged against big battered desks which looked as if, years ago, they had been on tour in one of Edgar Wallace's plays about Scotland Yard. There were no means of telling which orifice of the labyrinth one should enter; there were no signs of a porter. "*Alarmed*" (I saw myself, in the role of a half-baked foreign journalist, writing) *"alarmed by the rush to emigrate, Britain is making the process as unattractive and difficult as she can."*

Within an hour I was to remember this passing thought with shame.

"Any chance of a porter?"

"Be plenty soon, Sir." The policeman, too, was apple-cheeked and built on the lines of a butler. Almost immediately a porter appeared, a very nice man. "Just follow me, Sir." Off we went.

As a traveller I live in a world of my own. Because at one stage of my career I put in a certain amount of time crossing forbidden frontiers in remote regions, I tend—it is an odious trait—to regard the small, tiresome formalities of civilised travel with a weary but tolerant disdain. In truth, a certain arrogance underlies my approach to the problem of getting myself from A to B. Because normal travel is beset by none of the extremer hazards, because there will be no foundered camels, no dried-up water-holes, I embark on it in a negligent and rather condescending manner. I do not check my tickets, memorise my flight number, ensure that my vaccination certificate is not out of date, or take any of the minor, sensible precautions that better-adjusted voyagers take. I richly deserve the contretemps in which I am frequently involved.

As we approached the immigration corral I reached into my overcoat pocket for my passport. Funny thing, I could have sworn it was in the right-hand pocket. . . .

"Porter," I heard myself bleating a moment later in a foundered-camel voice, "you'd better dump the luggage here for the time being. I seem to have lost my passport. And my ticket."

The apple-cheeked policeman took it well.

"You think it may be in the taxi, Sir?" He ruminated, screwing up his eyes. "JXY249 . . . or was it 248? I saw you arrive. I'm pretty sure it's 249. We'll see what can be done."

He moved towards a dark-blue telephone.

"Or it might be in the train," I said. "The last time I saw it was in the train."

The train, it appeared, would now be on its way to Weymouth. The constable would get the CID at Bournemouth to investigate this possibility. I had the illusion of being a bit-player in that Edgar Wallace play.

The taxi was located and searched. At Bournemouth the prosperous couple who had shared my compartment remembered me getting out at Southampton; but I had not left my passport behind. It had vanished.

As I shambled up the gangway a few minutes before the ship sailed (for, rather surprisingly, I was allowed to take passage in her) I wondered for what particular act of hubris the gremlins had punished me. In future, I vowed, I would take more care not to provoke them. If at any later stage of a complicated journey I find myself adopting a *de haut en bas* attitude to the unexotic procedures of civilised travel I shall put my hand in my pocket and call myself to order by touching my passport. Provided, of course, that I get another one.

Though only fifteen years senior to the Queen Mary, the liner is obsolete and is due to be broken up. To the layman it seems surprising that you cannot sell a ship as a floating concern, or anyhow that you get more money for her if you take her to pieces and sell the masts and the mirrors, the refrigerators and the anchors, the ping-pong tables and the ash-trays and the planks out of the deck, in separate lots. But there it is.

A slight air of doom hangs over the first-class accommodation. I think this is due not so much to the liner's impending dissolution as to the fact that there is only a handful of first-class passengers. The stewards permanently on duty in the lounge and the bar and the library man their posts with a listless air, like sentries outside the palace of a discredited dictator. The band, tirelessly dispensing melodies from *Oklahoma!* and *Bless the Bride*, generally outnumbers its audience. There is something unreal and vaguely haggard about the ritual of "Tea-Time Melodies," a regular feature in the day's tastefully printed Programme of Events; it is as though the innumerable chairs had almost all been emptied by a plague, and the musicians are making a brave, hopeless attempt to keep up the spirits of the survivors.

Things are different in the Tourist Class, which is packed with 600 passengers including a contingent of Hungarians. These, sad to say, are not liked by those who minister to their needs and who find them exigent, querulous and dirty. One complaint, to my mind more frivolous than the rest, is that the Hungarians refuse to pay for their deck-chairs. It has always been a mystery to me why shipping companies, who provide their passengers with sofas, settees, armchairs, music, card-tables, chess-boards, mural paintings and even a newspaper, should charge them ten shillings for the use of a deck-chair and five shillings for the pillows and rugs that go with it. But I expect it is a very old maritime custom.

On this voyage the company's revenue from deck-chairs must have been negligible, for halfway across the Atlantic we ran into a violent storm. The wind was Force 11 (Force 12, I believe, is a hurricane) and for two days our speed was reduced from fifteen knots to less than five. The old ship groaned and juddered. It seemed to be full of the ghosts of plump Edwardian cooks lowering themselves into wickerwork armchairs. The walls of my cabin emitted such sounds as Jonah must have heard when the whale ground its teeth. The sea looked splendid. In the end we were more than two days late.

Now I have left the ship. Another traveller occupies my place at the Captain's table, scans the huge breakfast menu, toys ineffectually with the idea of ordering waffles or onion soup, is served almost too attentively by the soft-voiced steward who knows Mr. Noël Coward, studies the unfamiliar and sometimes scarcely credible names of the lady novelists with whose works the ship's library is largely stocked, paces the promenade deck, listens (I hope) to the band. I do not, to be frank, envy him very much, because I get bored at sea; but I cannot pity him either, for at least he possesses a passport.

THE LAUGHING-STOCK OF LOAMSHIRE

I HARDLY believe that the thing that happened to me the week before last could have happened to anybody else. One of the reasons for my disbelief is that, unlike most people, I have no sense of smell. Other reasons will suggest themselves as I slice off the *tranche de vie*.

I was shooting with my friend R. W. in the once fashionable county of Loamshire. (Imaginary counties, like imaginary kingdoms, have rather come down in the world. Ruritania, converted from a romantic duelling ground to an ideological abattoir, retains—like the ruins of a folly upon which solemn masques are staged—a certain functional *raison d'être*; but I fear we have heard almost the last of Loamshire.)

In front of R. W.'s house there is a large lake, frequented by mallard, widgeon, teal, pochard, shoveller, tufted duck and other wildfowl. When we returned from shooting the coverts he suggested that we should go down to some hides on the shores of the lake and see whether in the last of the December twilight the duck, which had been disturbed that morning, were flighting in again.

My hide, which I shared with my dog, was a small platform built out over the shallows and surrounded by boskage; access was by a rickety plank. One of the secrets of flighting duck in a failing light is to watch the sky almost straight above you; for although visibility seems no worse in lower and more normal sectors of your field of vision, it is in fact only when they are almost directly overhead that you will see the black shapes hurtling in the sky.

For a quarter of an hour I gazed intently upwards. I had killed a singleton mallard soon after taking my place in the hide, but although the upper air was occasionally cleft by the whicker of unseen wings, the other guns were getting little shooting and it was clear that not much was going to happen before the dusk yielded to the darkness. From the rising ground above the lake orange rectangles in the windows of the house presaged tea, and warmth.

But I was content with the grey, dank, expectant moment of English time in which I was stationed, and hoped that our host would not call us in too soon. It was only when I became aware of a sort of haze or miasma emanating from the hide that I relaxed my vigilance and ceased to stare vertically upwards into the slate-coloured void. My first thought was that my dog's wet coat was steaming. I was still trying to square this idiotic notion with my knowledge that he must be as cold as I was when I realised that, whether cold or not, I was on fire.

Haze or miasma my foot! What had tardily caught my attention (and had, I learnt later, for some minutes past been gravely offending the nostrils of the next gun, two hundred yards away downwind) was dense smoke arising from a conflagration in the left-hand pocket of my jacket. The fire had been started by dottle from my pipe; a box of safety matches had provided it with fuel; and the fact that I always have the pockets of shooting-jackets lined with rubber, to keep the cartridges dry, explains why the next gun was feeling the need for a respirator.

The obvious thing to do was to take the coat off and extinguish the cheery little glow in my pocket; but in order to do this I needed to put my gun down. This was not feasible inside the hide, where there was only about as much room as there is in a telephone kiosk and where the dog might easily have jolted the gun off the little platform into the water. So I stepped on to the rickety plank and made for the shore.

As soon as I left the shelter of the hide I met the full force of the wind; and although this was only a stiff breeze it naturally caused the fire to burn more briskly than before. When I reached the bank and got the coat off I found that my tweed knickerbockers had also begun to smoulder. I beat out this fresh outbreak with my left hand while with my right hand I lowered the jacket, hissing, into the dark waters of the lake. Though I lost a fountain-pen in the process, the situation was soon restored and I made my way up to the house, shaking with uncontrollable laughter like a character in a novel by Mr. Dornford Yates.

Afterwards, thinking it over during a long drive home, it slowly dawned on me that the episode—which, though ridiculous, I saw as a perfectly natural occurrence with more than a touch of inevitability about it—might appear to other people in a different light. The other guns had indeed laughed politely when I showed them my charred and sodden jacket; but what were they saying now?

". . . And it was a rubber pocket. *Rubber*, mark you!

George was a good two hundred yards away, and he swears he was damn near feeling queasy from the stink. Strix *says* he hasn't got a sense of smell. But, well, I mean to say, a chap simply can't be on fire and not notice it for all that length of time. He'd burnt a socking great hole in his trousers, too. If you ask me, the poor old boy's pretty well round the bend."

I had, sadly, to admit to myself that this would be the world's verdict, that I emerged from the business as a crazy old buffer, like the Absent-Minded Professor in back numbers of *Punch* but without a scholar's excuse for being in the clouds.

However, it was too late now to do anything about it; and I comforted myself with the reflection that, although to be the laughing-stock of Loamshire is not quite on a par with contributing to the gaiety of nations, my life had been enriched by an experience which, however you look at it, is not the sort of thing that happens to people every day.

THE DANGERS OF DOODLING

TÊTE-À-TÊTE

A. Extract from a Despatch, dated April 11, 1957, to the Foreign Office from HM Ambassador in Strelsau.

. . . Accordingly, without waiting for instructions, I demanded to see the Foreign Minister, who acceded to my request for an interview with more promptitude than is his wont. . . . M. Parolles (who appeared to me to have aged considerably under the strain of the past three weeks) was wholly unable, and indeed scarcely attempted, to justify his Government's decision to requisition for use as a military brothel the premises hitherto occupied by the British Council; and when I raised the question of adequate compensation he evaded the issue, which he attempted to obscure by quoting an old Ruritanian proverb. I took the opportunity of suggesting that neither indecency nor irrelevance were the surest corner-stones on which to build the foundations of a new Anglo-Ruritanian understanding; and, after briefly adumbrating the scope (though not, I need hardly say, the nature) of the measures which Her Majesty's Government might feel themselves obliged to adopt in the face of continued Ruritanian intransigence, I look my leave.

Throughout our conversation M. Parolles's ears were twitching more violently than usual, and I feel bound to modify the scepticism expressed in my dispatch (X/YZ 21227 of 17 March, 1957: *Account of Official Reception in honour of Mr. R. H. S. Crossman and the Lutterworth Trumpet-Majorettes*) concerning recent rumours about his state of health. . . .

B. Extract from a Report, dated April 11, 1957, to the Dux of Ruritania from his Secretary of State for Foreign Affairs.

. . . The British Ambassador's request for an interview had been couched in peremptory terms, and on his arrival at the Foreign Ministry I arranged for him to be kept waiting for three-quarters of an hour. . . . Sir Hector's manner was agitated; I formed the impression that he is, or soon will be, on the verge of a nervous breakdown. The almost hysterical vehemence with which he protested against our action in terminating the lease of No. 43 Zilliacuplast provided further confirmation that our suspicions about the so-called "British Council" were correct and that the building has in fact been used as a centre of espionage and subversion. . . . When Sir Hector attempted to argue that his Government were entitled to some monetary compensation, I took the opportunity of reminding him of our old proverb about the virgin and the louse. Although, like all his countrymen, deficient in a sense of humour, Sir Hector seemed disconcerted by my *jeu d'esprit*, and launched into a tirade—obviously intended to be minatory—in which such phrases as "view with grave concern," "seriously impair the fabric of" and "appropriate measures" recurred. . . . I terminated the interview by saying that I had urgent matters to discuss with the Guatemalan Chargé d'Affaires. It is charitable to ascribe to the alcoholism of which he is notoriously a victim the altogether pathetic manner in which the Ambassador made his *démarche*. . . .

Wait For It

"I am told," began our host; then broke off to relume his cigar.

The huge lighter, raised suddenly into prominence from among the rest of the silver on the dinner table, was revealed as a sort of pretender-cruet, a vulgarian attached to a regiment in whose ranks it would remain always on probation. We guessed that it had been presented to its owner, in a warm boardroom, by his colleagues and subordinates.

"I am told," he repeated.

As the docile bulbous flame expanded and contracted round the end of his cigar, the words floated about us in the contrived moment of suspense. They had been spoken with an offhand unction; we guessed the speaker to be very near the centre of affairs. His tone conjured up a vision of influential hands being laid on his sleeve as he prepared to enter a *salon*, of the CIGS's Rolls crackling the gravel of his Surrey drive on a Sunday afternoon, of notes, scribbled on the back of order papers, converging on the Distinguished Strangers' Gallery when he appeared in it.

His tone was not pontifical; it was weighty, measured, authoritative. He would not—he probably could not—tell us all. He was unlikely to be indiscreet. We listened, nevertheless, expectantly.

"I am told," said our host, his great face wreathed in smoke like an idol's in incense, "that the Government is far from happy about the international situation."

He paused.

"*Very* far from happy," he repeated. He put his enormous lighter back on the table with a small, but incisive, thud, and relapsed into silence.

CONCEDING A POINT

"But at least," urged the minor politician's friend, "his last speech had a certain cogency?"

The minor politician's enemy made a small, guileful gesture of assent and said:

"His utterances are always distinguished by the quality you mention. But the note struck is irrelevant, shrill and unavailing. His most cogent speeches remind me of nothing so much as the whistle of a passing locomotive which intrudes upon the broadcast description of a Test Match."

"Of course," he added, glancing sideways at the first speaker and infusing into his voice a note of generosity, "such interventions hardly matter if nothing much is happening at the time."

MANLY RESIGNATION

"Being cuckolded," said the cavalry officer, "is like going bald. By the time you realise it is happening, it is too late to do very much about it."

ELEVENPENCE

I COULD not help being deeply interested by something that happened recently at York. The central figure in this incident was a forty-one-year-old burglar. At his trial he asked for five other offences to be taken into consideration, so he can hardly be regarded as a complete amateur in crime. He was sent to prison for five years.

At the time of his arrest his swag amounted to elevenpence. If a film or a play were based on his crime, there can be no two opinions about who would get the leading part; it would go to Mr. Robertson Hare. For this poor burglar broke into the dormitory of a girls' school. Its five occupants attacked him. "Because" (according to *The Times*) "he was in his stockinged feet he slipped on the highly polished floor"; and four of the girls "detained him by sitting on him" while the fifth fetched help.

We all make mistakes, we all have our failures; but if we have tenacity and a measure of luck, we generally manage to redeem them in the end. The mistaken diagnosis, the missed cue, the dropped catch, the lost battle, the booed first night, the judgment tartly reversed on appeal—at the time these lapses darken our lives; we feel that our careers have ended in the pillory. But if we press on regardless, they are forgotten or forgiven by the world, and perhaps in our own minds are transmuted from an inexpressibly painful memory to a story that—suitably edited—we tell against ourselves.

It is somehow difficult to believe that the burglar's experiences in the dormitory will ever be sublimated in this way. Prisons, I believe, are more humane places than they used to be, but one feels instinctively that what is left of this burglar's *amour-propre* is bound to be further eroded in general conversation with his fellow inmates. If only he had had a tiara or two in his pocket when he was sat upon, if only he had been sat upon by débutantes. . . . But *elevenpence*! And *schoolgirls*! If anything is calculated to make a felon go straight, it is having to admit to other felons, at intervals spread over five years, that such were the ingredients of his last attempt at crime.

This particular felon, though a model of incompetence, is not all bad. "He had," said Counsel at his trial, "at least some feelings of humanity, for he has written to the court saying that he intends to plead Guilty and asking that the girls should not have to spoil the holidays they have just begun by being called to give evidence." Chivalry is rare these days, but this is it. We are not quite on the level of Sidney Carton, but at least the poor man's humiliations did not breed in him a spirit of vindictiveness. He was about to lose five years of his freedom; it was decent of him to show concern lest his captors should lose one day of theirs.

But what of the other actors in this drama? What of the heroines? Nurtured (one fears) mainly on the works of Miss Enid Blyton, but partly (one hopes) on those of Mr. Arthur Ransome, they have no doubt always half-expected to be involved in some desperate adventure. Are they, now that all the excitement is over, tasting faintly the flavour of disillusion, of anti-climax? Are they already beginning to suspect that fact, though often stranger than fiction, is never quite as *tidily* dramatic, that it almost always contains an element of bathos or incongruity, that there is often only elevenpence in the marauder's pocket? And what did they talk about, as they sat in a row on the burglar like nannies on a bench in the Park?

These are, alas, imponderable questions. With more

111

certainty, and with much pleasure, we can reflect on all the beneficial by-products of that brief, tense struggle in the dormitory. How greatly it will simplify the task of the principal speaker next speech day! How much it will enrich the legends of five different families! One can hear echoes of the episode reverberating, faint but clear, far into the twenty-first century. "Grannie, is it true that once when you were at school you sat on a burglar?" "Yes, dear," Grannie will say, looking gratified; and after recapitulating at some length recent intelligence about the careers of her collaborators ("I always said she was mad to marry a missionary. . . . Insisted on moving to *Droitwich*, of all places. . . . 'Backward' is putting it *very* mildly") she will launch upon an account of her great adventure. In such matters ladies are perhaps less given to boasting, embroidering and romancing than men, and no doubt Grannie's story will be substantially accurate. But something tells me that by then one detail will have been forgotten, omitted or suppressed; we shall have lost the elevenpence.

THE BRITISH NIHILISTS

THE other day I put through a transatlantic telephone call to my home in England from a place in New Brunswick.

"I'll call you back," said the friendly, courteous voice of the Canadian girl on the exchange. Presently she did.

"I'm sorry, caller," she said, "but London says there's no such number as Scribblebury 304. Are you sure that's the number you want?"

I said I was quite sure; it was my own telephone number and had been for twenty years.

"OK," said the girl cheerfully. "We'll try again."

London spoke in a lugubrious Cockney snarl. "I've told you, miss, there's no such number. . . . No, the line's not out of order; it's simply that there's no such *number*. . . . Directory Inquiries? They can't 'elp unless they 'ave the full name and address of the subscriber your caller wishes to be connected with. . . . Oh, very well. . . . 'Ow do you spell that?"

Tetchily, with an ill grace, London took down the particulars; and eventually came back to say that there was a subscriber called Strix on the Scribblebury exchange—Scribblebury 304.

"That's the number I asked for," said the Canadian girl, still friendly, still courteous.

"Oh no it wasn't," London retorted. "You asked me for 344. Do you want this other number now?"

"Please." A minute later I got my connection.

Throughout the colloquy of which I have given a much condensed summary the contrast between the two operators was so marked that it was difficult to believe that they shared a common purpose, were collaborating in the same enterprise. The Canadian girl sounded throughout as if she actively *wanted* me to get my number; the Cockney sounded exactly the opposite. It was not merely that he didn't care a damn whether I got the number or not; he wanted the project, once he had proclaimed it impossible, to prove so.

In these islands we have become in recent years inured to this mild form of nihilism. "Typical!" we exclaim perfunctorily (and unfairly, for it is not typical and is, at a guess, getting rarer) when somebody tells us a hard-luck story of their treatment by a petty official, a shop assistant, a waitress, or some such. The burden of the victim's lament is almost always the same; he or she has come up against a brick wall in which bad manners supply the mortar and of which the foundations are laid, not so much in a positive desire to obstruct or humiliate, as in a drab, instinctive denial of sympathy and co-operation.

The reason why the surliness—apart from the inefficiency—of my compatriot on the telephone exchange made at the time such a strong impression on me was because, after travelling for two or three weeks in Canada, I had got out of the habit of half-expecting that sort of thing. My itinerary had been complicated, its tempo urgent. It had bristled with small administrative anxieties. A preternaturally early breakfast, a suit pressed overnight, a railroad reservation altered at short notice, an air passage confirmed or reconfirmed, a suitcase brought from the checkroom to a rendezvous—each was in itself a trivial transaction.

Yet almost every day there had been some small, boring task which needed to be performed for me with alacrity by a stranger, and failure in which would have jeopardised my chances of getting from A to B, and on to C and D, in time. There was no failure, nor was there anything in the Canadian atmosphere to suggest that there might be one. I know nothing at all about Canada; but I have the impression that the people of that country are actively concerned to further any reasonable enterprise, whether it is supervising a truce in Indo-China or making sure that a traveller catches his train. They do not *enjoy* saying "You've had it, chum"; they never say "I couldn't care less."

I am against blaming things on wars. Indeed, I am against anyone blaming things on anything outside himself, even if he has some right to, because it never does him any good in the long run. But I suspect that it was in the immediate aftermath of the last war that British nihilism first became a noticeable part of the national climate.

114

Nihilism ("negative doctrines, total rejection of current beliefs, in religion or morals": *OED*) is really too grandiose, too positive a word to describe the attitude I have in mind. A flaccid unhelpfulness, an ulcerous *satyagraha*, a form of apathy which places upon small rules and regulations the same sort of reliance that a blowsy woman places upon corsets—these are among its unbecoming symptoms.

I often wonder where we got it from and why a minority of the population appears, in the discharge of its duties, to model its conduct on the less well-adjusted type of Bengali stationmaster. Whence comes that note of sour relish in the tones in which they tell us that it is too late to get a meal, too early to get a drink, that the 10.48 has since the beginning of the month left at 10.32, that now the next train will be at 2.35, that Mr. Smith is out, that they do not know where he has gone, or for how long, or whether he is coming back to the office at all today or is likely to be in tomorrow. . . .

The British, whatever their other faults, are not a cruel or even a deliberately unkind race. Why do they take it out of each other in this way? It could be, of course, that the nihilists are so lacking in perception that they are unaware of the blight they cast, the disappointment and irritation which they engender; but there is often a faint gleam in their stony eyes, a slight edge on their lacklustre voices, which suggest that they know perfectly well what they are about.

They are arbitrarily as well as sparsely distributed. One may go for days or weeks without encountering them, moving through a world of sunny dispositions in which everybody is out to help everybody else. But in the end one log turns out to be a crocodile, and once more one is up against the glassy stare, the dank, chilling indifference, the general attitude of a-responsibility.

I suppose the nihilists have always been with us. I suppose that a truly progressive person would recognise them as the victims of some psychic maladjustment, as objects for sympathy.

I am afraid I cannot go as far as this myself. The nearest I can get to taking a charitable view of them is to wish that they would go and live in some other country.

CENTURY

FACTS are wonderful things. I wish my mind held a larger store of them. I should like, occasionally, to be able to correct or even controvert statements made by other people, to lean forward and to say quietly: "But surely you mean eighteen ninety *five*? The exact date, if I remember rightly, was the 26th of April," or "No, no, my dear fellow. Cubic *metres*, not cubic yards. You forget that they were relying on Portuguese statistics." I cannot recall ever making an intervention of this kind.

People like me, people with empty heads, have a wistful regard for facts. But, human nature being what it is, those who present facts to us are often aware, as they warm to their theme, of a certain abstraction in our manner which may develop into something not far removed from sullenness. If you were to watch us being (say) taken round a factory you would observe a progressive deterioration in our attitude. The alert, intelligent exclamations of "Is it really?", "*How* many tons did you say?" and "Astonishing!" with which we began the tour, give way to more perfunctory comments, like "Oh, I see" or even "Oh." By the end we are barely grunting, and as we take our departure a minor executive comes running after us with the illustrated brochure, the last annual report, and the three recent issues of the house magazine which we thought we had unobtrusively jettisoned under a huge leather armchair in the managing director's office. We thank him with a glazed, guilty smile.

This unenlightened attitude is due in most cases, and certainly in mine, to a feeling of hopelessness. I know that the facts are going in at one ear and out at the other, that none of them will stick in my head, that it is simply no *good* my trying to remember what they said about the relation between the number of revolutions per minute registered on the dial of the Hartley-Gilmour counter-stabilising unit and the over-all throughput per man-shift.

But apart from this well-justified defeatism there is a baser element, the element of envy; to me these facts, flowing so copiously, marshalled with such precision, are in effect sour grapes. I do not envy them as possessions, but I envy the power to possess them. Thus, on the London pavements, is a man in evening dress envied by some sour and drably plumaged loiterer.

There is, however, one type of fact-monger whom I admire unreservedly. A representative of this sub-species is to be found, surrounded by works of reference, in a garret under the roof of the building from which the *Spectator* is edited. His counterpart exists on every newspaper.

The man who takes you round a factory, or explains the political situation in Siam or the problems connected with the licensing of whelk-stalls, is like a heron feeding its young; he is regurgitating. Charles Seaton in his garret is quite different. He is like a well-trained hawk. You fly him at facts as you fly a hawk at game. He knows a great many facts already; but no one in his position can have at his finger-tips the answers to all the questions he is liable to be asked by his colleagues, or even a rough idea of the fields of knowledge which the questions are liable to cover. His duty is not to parade facts which are already on the strength, but to go out into no man's land and bring back a prisoner.

Beings of this kind are the only true masters of facts. The expert, the specialist, the scholar is really their slave. He may, indeed he generally does, enjoy his slavery. When a new book on his subject appears, or a great wad of new statistics, he swoops on it as avidly as a pigeon on a crop of peas; his erudition steadily grows.

But he is like a ringmaster in a circus. At the crack of his whip the facts circulate obediently, tossing their manes, raising their trunks in salute. Although, however, ponies and elephants can exist without a ring-master, a ringmaster cannot exist without ponies and elephants. It is rather the same with facts; the greater your dominance over them, the more you depend on them.

In Charles Seaton's field facts are a quarry to be hunted down, captured and given away: not an ever-expanding menagerie to be tended. The greatest Master of Fact-Hounds that I know is J. S. Maywood, who has served *The Times* for fifty years, the last forty-four of them as head of their Intelligence Department. When you confront him with some hideously recondite question his meditative "Let me *see* . . ." is like a distant view-halloo, and as he strides swiftly off into a labyrinth of shelves and filing cabinets, gazetteers and Greek lexicons, you have vaguely the impression that he is tightening his girths and ramming his hat down more firmly on his head.

A bright, predatory gleam comes into the eyes of such men when you ask them apologetically on which day of the week the Battle of Bannockburn was fought, whence the Isle of Purbeck got its title to insularity, or in what

118

year the Martini-Henry was taken into service in the British Army. They are outfitters in omniscience, purveyors of the authoritative touch. Occasionally one can recognise the fruits of their backroom labours in such expressions as "of course" ("*it was not, of course, until the following year that Paraguay decided to adhere to the Convention*"), "incidentally" ("*the Regional Committees, incidentally, do not seem to have been asked for their views at this stage*") and "it is too often forgotten/ sometimes overlooked/ not generally realised" ("*that the frontier agreement of 1920 was never ratified by either signatory*"). When I read sentences of this kind in serious newspapers, I salute, with gratitude and respect, the hidden hand of the fact-master.

It was not about the fact-master, but about one particular fact, that I intended to write this article; for it is the hundredth of its kind that I have contributed to the *Spectator* since, just over two years ago, the mantle of Sir Harold Nicolson and Sir Compton Mackenzie descended on me, like a rich bandanna dislodged from the still-room shelf upon a transient mouse.

But weekly journalism has few affinities with cricket. To lean negligently on one's pen and to raise one's cap in acknowledgement of the tumultuous applause is, I suppose, possible: perhaps even seemly. But then one would have to supply the tumultuous applause oneself, and the more I examined the project the more arch and otiose it appeared. So, since I should not have known that I had notched a hundred if Charles Seaton had not told me, it seemed fairer, and more agreeable, to write an article about him.

LIKEE UTOPIA?

"THESE'LL do," said the nice man who was showing me round. We took our places in two chairs marked respectively NORWAY and CUBA.

The eleven members of the Security Council sit in a horseshoe. Each delegate has a little squad of three or four advisers grouped tightly behind him, like seconds huddling round a boxer's corner after the bell has ordered them out of the ring. On the wall behind the President a vast mural painting by a Scandinavian artist symbolises "the promise of future peace and individual freedom." Opposite this—opposite the open end of the horseshoe—rise the public benches. These were packed. High up under the ceiling on either side are two rows of small windows. Behind one row the interpreters discharge with an uncanny precision their never-ending task; the other windows are the eyes and ears of the press and radio, and in one of them a red light now came on as a television camera focused on Sir Firoz Khan Noon, who began to read, not particularly well, a statement about Kashmir.

Fastened to our chairs were tiny microphones attached to concave plastic containers rather like small soap-dishes. You fit the container over one ear and regulate by means of a switch the language in which you receive the speech. You have a choice of five—English, French, Spanish, Russian and Chinese—and if you were dexterous enough and had a good ear you could I suppose in time acquire quite a large vocabulary in any of these languages; for the interpreters are always a shade behind the speakers, and by switching quickly from Channel 1 to Channel 5 you would soon become master of the Chinese for "totally inadmissible," "ulterior motives," "colonialism run riot" and others of the phrases with which the path towards world government is paved.

Neither Pakistan nor India is at present a member of the Security Council, but both had been invited to present their views on this old Kashmir quarrel; on the previous day a Russian veto had blocked one line of approach to its settlement, and now, at the instance of America and Britain, a slightly different formula was being considered. So when Sir Firoz Khan Noon had finished his (as I thought) moderate and even conciliatory discourse, it was Mr. Khrishna Menon's turn.

Mr. Menon is an actor. His performances do not always endear him to the other members of the cast, or even to the audience; but it is impossible to deny him star quality. A day or two earlier he had collapsed in mid-harangue, and a grey-haired doctor now sat solicitously at his elbow. With just the hint of a stagger Mr. Menon rose to ask, on a note of righteous indignation, for a recess. The last thing he wanted to do was to waste the Security Council's time, but the observations of the delegate for Pakistan had been so tendentious and misleading that he felt obliged to prepare a refutation instead of (as he had intended) merely restating India's position in formal terms. He wanted a quarter of an hour in which to limber up.

The Security Council clearly quailed at this prospect. While they canvassed the matter, a feeling of being personally anomalous left me. At first this feeling had been strong. Here I was, smoking a pipe on a chair marked NORWAY, quite possibly nestling abaft Sir Firoz Khan Noon's left ear on millions of television screens. A few moments earlier Sir Pierson Dixon had left his corner of the ring to exchange words with me. As far as I could see there was nothing to stop me from writing on the back of an envelope, "*Formosa is being invaded. Mr. Tsiang is wanted urgently on the telephone*," passing it to the cheerful Chinese understrapper in front of me, and then, with a few deprecating nods and bows, moving forward to occupy China's seat on the Security Council.

It would have needed a more brazen, an otherwise-adjusted character to put my *sens du praticable* to the test. But meanwhile I had found my own level as a non-combatant in the curious arena in which the world's conscience plays under a fierce limelight the same central and absolutely indispensable part as the rope does in a tug-of-war. I was not in a council chamber; I was on a stage, trespassing among the players like the snuff-taking gallants who insisted on carrying their stools into the wings of the Restoration theatres.

But this was no ordinary stage, and these were no ordinary actors. For one thing, they were all playing to different audiences. When the Russian delegate rose to announce that he would abstain from voting on the amendment (thus making it reasonably certain that it would be carried), he was not seeking to impress the serried tiers of tourists and schoolgirls who looked down on him, or even his distinguished colleagues round the horseshoe table. He was merely doing what his government, for inscrutable reasons, had told him to do. He was striking an attitude on its behalf. Perhaps he and the others were puppets first, actors only incidentally.

It is widely assumed that the UN is ineffective because it is bisected by an ideological gulf; if it went into liquidation tomorrow, *nyet* would be its epitaph in the minds of disappointed idealists. But if the Iron Curtain and all it stands for did not exist, if there were only the normal interplay of self-interest and mutual distrust, the normal incompatibilities of race and religion and national outlook, surely the United Nations would still be crippled by the fallacy on which its charter is based —the fallacy that human affairs are best regulated, not by negotiation, but by passing public resolutions and striking moral attitudes? Especially if the resolutions cannot be enforced, especially if the attitudes are often patently insincere.

There are doubtless several reasons why the Americans are on the whole more disposed than we are to take the United Nations seriously. One of them—perhaps not the least cogent—is that a great many Americans, besides knowing the delegates as television personalities, have seen and explored the 39-storey steel and glass building on the bank of the East River which houses the UN headquarters. All day long conducted tours troop round its spacious corridors, throng the Gift Shop, and scrutinise the exhibits in a sort of embryo museum; these include blow-pipes and fish-hooks from trusteeship territories, photographs of the earliest committees, instruments of ratification, and the first United Nations flag to be hoisted in Korea. In the crowded book-store the eyes of (one presumes) connoisseurs scan a wide range of titles: *The Place of Sport in Education: a Comparative Study, Protocole sur les Stupéfiants, Protein Malnutrition in Brazil, Supplementary Interpretations and Instructions for Coding Causes of Death, Education Politique des Femmes, Trade Union Rights in Czechoslovakia*—there is something for every taste.

Outside in the frosty sunlight a sixteen-foot-tall bronze Amazon holds aloft, despite the frenzied caracoling of her horse, an olive branch in one hand and a globe in the other; she symbolises peace, and was the gift of Yugoslavia. On the terraces cameras click and whir as the pilgrims immortalise their visit to the shrine. To them the United Nations Organisation will always be something more than the nebulous abstraction, the cue for platitudes on the one hand or music-hall jokes on the other, which it is to most of us. For them it represents a reality, like Niagara Falls.

Politeness demands that I should say that it now represents a reality for me, too; but I don't think that *reality* was the impression uppermost in my mind as I left the United States and, after crossing First Avenue in the van of a small, rather cosy anti-British demonstration carrying placards about Cyprus, made for the interior of the island.

CHAT AND WIMBLESTRAW

A NEW village is to be built on the scrofulous site of a hutted camp near Dorchester in Oxfordshire, and the problem of what to call it confronts the planning authorities in that county with a problem in several ways characteristic of our self-conscious and over-organised age. The Parish Council has plumped for Wimblestraw, a name which (according to the *Oxford Times*) "has a local connection in that it is the name of a type of grass once found in the area and of one of the enclosed pieces of land shown on the Tithe Map." This suggestion has been turned down at a higher level and "the debate" (the same paper observes) "grows each week more and more like that about the Oxford relief roads." The alternative names so far put forward include Colwell and New Bullingdon. Wimblestraw may be a shade arch, but it is surely better than either of these.

Once Wimblestraw, or whatever they decide to call the place, gets its name it will keep it; for village names are no longer subject to that mysterious process of evolution which could easily have converted a seventeenth-century Wimblestraw into a twentieth-century Wamblestream without anybody quite knowing why (and which did, for instance, over the same period transform a near-by village from Bensington to Benson). But even today the names of woods and fields and dwelling places—though not, I think, of hills or promontories or rivers—are all the time in a state of gentle, almost imperceptible flux which I find fascinating.

Dwelling places offer the most obvious but the least interesting example of this process at work. If some prosperous fellow buys a farm-labourer's cottage which has been known for generations as The Grubbings, a change of name is an improvement even more inevitable than concrete gnomes and an asbestos-roofed garage. The Grubbings becomes Shangri-la, Jaybeesden or Mitford End. What is more, the new name—as one says of inoculations—"takes." It finds its way into the telephone directory, the register of electors, the valuation officer's files and the tradesmen's books. True, it does not come trippingly off the tongue of the local inhabitants. "Ar, you mean Mr. Fatlock's place?" they say if asked by a car-load of his cronies to be directed to Shangri-la. But the old name dies and the new name lives.

It is different with woods and fields. Fields, I should suppose, are hardly ever deliberately renamed. But in the last twenty years the high-pressure modernisation of agriculture set in motion by the stresses of war has led to a sort of wholesale reshuffling of the pack. In some places hedges have been grubbed up and small fields thrown into larger ones. Elsewhere the opposite has happened. The perfect and absolute blank of OS 1001 (it is by the numbers allotted to them by the Ordnance Survey when the district was last mapped that fields are known to tax inspectors, tithe commissioners and other interested parties) has lost its immemorial status as The Sixty Acre and becomes a mosaic of barbed wire. Thus old names—which in any case often have only a precarious registry in the memories of the oldest men on the place—are tending to disappear and new names are being coined to fit a fresh pattern of enclosures.

"Being coined" suggests an act of conscious cerebration, the exercise of a choice, the taking of a decision; it is to that extent misleading. Farmers, unlike foresters, seldom attempt to be tidy-minded in these matters, and it often takes two or three years before a new field acquires a generally recognisable sobriquet of its own. The interregnum of anonymity is filled with time-wasting efforts to identify it. "When you've done, leave the roller in the farthest of those two fields on the far side of the old track. . . . No, *not* the one we had rape in last year. The other one. Remember where the muck-spreader stood over Easter after the wheel came off?" Most of these colloquies are carried on above the roar of a tractor engine; and I suspect that startling results would emerge from a time-and-motion study of the net loss to agricultural productivity directly attributable to nobody knowing what particular fields are called.

Field-names are not recorded by the Ordnance Survey; the names of woods are. Yet this does not always confer the firm and general currency that you might expect. Old woods normally retain their names intact, though sometimes the nicknames bestowed on them by the children of their owners survive to compete with the authorised version. But it is easier to give a new wood a name than to ensure that the name will be used. The 1912 edition of the Ordnance Survey showed five new plantations of about ten acres each which my grandfather had then recently established. Their names reflect the tastes and interests of his children: Kate's Copse (my grandmother was called Kate), Beagle Brake (my father kept a pack of bassets), Aintree Raise, Badger Bank, Top Copse and Chats Wood. All these names are still on the map, but not one of them is ever used—except, about once a year, by the Forestry Commission, who work from the Ordnance Survey when dealing with maintenance grants and the like.

I can remember Chat, of Chats Wood; memory grants to the animals in one's childhood an immortality which often unfairly eludes—unless they were outstandingly objectionable or ridiculous—the human bit-players in Act I. She was a fat, elderly, privileged West Highland terrier belonging to my grandmother. I suppose she used to hunt in "her" wood when she was a young dog and it was a young plantation (it was clear-felled in the last war and is now a young plantation again).

But I have never heard it called anything except Black Wood. For a long time I assumed that "Black" was a rather far-fetched corruption of "Chats" until I learnt from an old man that Black Wood was the name of the original field before it was planted up. A similar fate has overtaken Beagle Brake; indeed, the old field-name— Tyler's—has been debased, through much use by a game-keeper given to malapropism, to Tilehurst, which is the unlovely name of a Reading suburb. Of the six little woods which were new fifty years ago only Aintree Raise has retained a vicarious affinity with the name it was given; it is indeed called something quite different, but the field below it, where there used to be a gallop, is still known as The Jumps.

It must go on all over the country, this endless, un-declared war between new names and old names. Fresh associations, altered boundaries and personal whims are allies of the new names; the old names are often be-trayed by failing memories, blurred utterance and changes of ownership. Like all official historians, the Ordnance Survey gives us a belated and impersonal view of the conflict; and the only hope of a lacklustre peace lies with the Forestry Commission, to whom (though so far to no one else) the fifteen acres to which my grandmother's terrier owes her quasi-immortality are known as Compartment 26.

YOU NEVER KNOW

INCH by inch the frontiers of knowledge are advanced, the dark clouds of ignorance dispelled, mankind's torturing uncertainties allayed. Last week, after four years of endeavour, the United States Air Force "pinpointed Europe's position in relation to that of the North American continent."

In announcing this achievement Reuter's choice of a main verb might, one feels, have been more closely attuned to European susceptibilities. A tiny atoll or a sunken wreck—these you can pinpoint; a socking great land mass like ours would seem to deserve some ampler, some less condescending verb. Besides, it sounds rather silly.

Not half so silly, though, as the statement made by an official spokesman when revealing that the width of the North Atlantic had at last been definitely established. "The Air Force," said this booby, "would like to disclose whether the two continents are farther apart or nearer together than is supposed, but such information would be of great military value to Russia." The ocean's width remains a secret.

I am often struck by the amount of time and money devoted by governments, international organisations, local authorities, seats of learning and other bodies to investigating matters which seem to be, at best, of only secondary importance. I remember a few years ago reading in *The Times* that out of 1,200 Somersetshire children between the ages of three and fourteen only two-thirds had been present when their shoes were bought; and scarcely a week goes by without the fruits of some equally inane inquiry being made public. What I should like to organise would be an investigation into the whole mumbo-jumbo of security, of which the business about the Atlantic is an extreme but not untypical manifestation.

Most people can remember examples of the absurd lengths to which in the last war the requirements of military secrecy were extended. I recall once landing at Gibraltar after a nonstop flight from Cairo in an aircraft bound for England. The passengers, who were all officers in uniform, had undergone a rigorous scrutiny before we took off in the early hours of the morning. Our identity cards and movement orders had been examined; if we were carrying official documents the certificates authorising us to do so had been checked; our names, initials, ranks and even weights were recorded on the manifest of passengers. Yet at Gibraltar all these precautions were duplicated.

Even in Cairo the assumption underlying them—that one of us might be an enemy agent—was prohibitively far-fetched. It was hard enough for a *bona fide* British brigadier to get himself the necessary priority on a flight to the UK. The idea that even the most resourceful spy could perform all the feats of imposture, disguise, forgery and *pistonnage* which would have been essential prerequisites to emplaning at Cairo was ludicrous; and it was still more ludicrous to assume that official travellers who had been screened and given clearance in Cairo, and who would be screened again on arrival in the UK, required vetting in transit through Gibraltar.

As we stood in a weary and dishevelled queue waiting for our documents to be re-examined, one of us pointed this out to the security officer who was performing this duty.

"What *is* all this in aid of?" he asked. "If our papers weren't in order we shouldn't be on the plane. We haven't landed anywhere, so we must be the same lot of people who were allowed to leave Cairo this morning. Or is the theory that some dubious character may have joined us in mid-air?"

The security officer looked at him with owlish sagacity.

"You never know, sir," he said.

It is probably to the adoption of the "You never know" principle that most of the major idiocies committed in the name of security are due. And of course you never do know. In hard fact it is inconceivable that particulars of the width of the Atlantic would be "of great military value," or of any military value at all, to the Russian General Staff; but nobody in the Pentagon can *prove* this. It is no more than a reasonable assumption, and in the lynx-eyes of security to make any assumption implying that there are limits to the capabilities of the enemy's intelligence is the height of irresponsibility.

Hence—amid countless other instances—the urgent official warning addressed in 1940 to all parish magazines; their editors were told that, when describing entertainments organised for Servicemen stationed in the neighbourhood, they must on no account report the number of teas served. Hence an order issued to the Territorial Army about four years ago. This order authorised officers to visit, if they wished, their unit's mobilisation stores (i.e. the crated equipment held ready in the area where the unit would concentrate on mobilisation); but these sentimental journeys were to be made in civilian clothes.

"Regimental ties," the order concluded, "will NOT be worn."

It was at about the same period that Territorial officers, at the best of times a sorely tried section of the community, were ordered to carry identity cards. To these had to be affixed a photograph of the bearer in uniform; but before this photograph could be taken the sitter's uniform had to be divested of "any badges or other insignia disclosing the Arm of the Service, Regiment, Corps, Department, formation or unit" to which he belonged.

Possibly Mr. Ian Fleming could tell us how much a Russian Assistant Military Attaché would pay a keen Communist for purloining an identity card belonging to Major J. P. T. Snooks of Muckton Hall, Loamshire

(a) if in the accompanying photograph the cap-badge of the Loamshire Regiment could be distinguished, or

(b) if it couldn't.

I should be the last to disparage the military importance of Major Snooks, or of the Territorial battalion of the Loamshires, or of the Territorial Army as a whole; but I should not seriously expect the Assistant Military Attaché to go much higher than a packet of cigarettes for either exhibit.

He might bid a shade more for the width of the Atlantic Ocean. You never know.

GUILTY SPLENDOUR

A whiff of guilty splendour goes with the possession of a swimming-pool. It is an un-English amenity. Though congruous to California, it has in these islands all the less pleasing attributes of a folly: ostentation without whimsicality, an air of purpose without the capacity to fulfil it, hideous expense without the addition of beauty to the landscape. A grotto or a ten-ton abstract by Mr. Henry Moore might be equally controversial; but neither would conjure up those visions of gooseflesh on starlets' thighs, of cigar-ash flaking down on to suede shoes after luncheon on Sunday near Maidenhead, that a swimming-pool does.

I built mine seven years ago. It is 20 yards long and 10 yards wide, holds 70,000 gallons of water and cost £503. It was made by the workmen on my estate after some excavation had been done by a contractor with a huge, yellow machine which kept on breaking down. The first 70,000 gallons of water we put into it (through a garden hose attached to a tap in the pantry) leaked, almost imperceptibly, out, and when this happened there was considerable chagrin.

We saw ourselves being left with a sort of concrete annexe to the lawn which, although a modified form of squash could be played in it, resembled nothing so much as the launching-site of a V1. But the walls were rendered again with a slightly different integument, and a week or so later (for it takes the pantry tap a long time to exgurgitate 70,000 gallons) the swimming-pool was full.

The following general observations may be of interest to any madcap who contemplates following my example:

Size. Experience suggests that I was wise to build a large pool. Apart from its obvious advantages to swimmers, children can, with the help of a small canvas dinghy or coracle, learn to row on a large pool; it is indeed surprising how much watermanship they acquire. And in a hard winter it is better to have a small skating rink than a microscopic one.

Hygiene. For £503 you cannot build a proper modern swimming-pool into which fresh (and very cold) water is continually pumped through a filter. Mine is simply a huge, static tank. It is emptied once a year, in the spring, when the bottom is found to be coated with a sediment vaguely resembling gooseberry fool. This is removed in buckets, and for perhaps a fortnight the refilled pool remains limpid. But, despite various patent chemicals which we throw in whenever anyone thinks of it, the water gradually becomes opaque and for the next eleven months its surface remains a sort of greenish khaki. This looks insalubrious but has not proved so.

Site. Our swimming-pool is only a few feet from the front of the house. This propinquity has many advantages. We can dive in whenever we feel like it, so that a swim does not involve a minor expedition and on a hot day can be repeated *ad lib.* in the intervals of doing something else. But it has disadvantages, too, and this brings me to the question of:

Honorary Members. It would be worse than churlish to restrict the use of one's swimming-pool by one's friends and neighbours and their children; but there are inevitably times, in hot weather, when I find myself wishing that the swimming-pool was less closely integrated to the house, that the continuous hullabaloo which rises from it did not rise directly below the window of my study, and that the many delightful people who come to swim could somehow be persuaded all to come at the same time. But it is too late to do anything about this now.

DANGER. A swimming-pool-owner with small children will find himself, soon after its construction has been completed, faced with demands that the pool shall be surrounded with some form of child-proof fence. No such thing exists; if it did it would be unsightly as well as expensive. A policy of evasion and procrastination is recommended. Falling into a swimming-pool is a character-building experience for non-swimmers, and my youngest daughter, who did this at the age of three during a snowstorm, has never been any the worse for it.

WILD LIFE. Swimming-pools are much appreciated by pied wagtails and swallows, but for some mysterious reason exert on tame owls a fatal fascination. At the moment our pool is going through a spell of mallard-trouble. Two years ago my keeper reared three broods of mallard on a pond half a mile from the house. In their first season they were so tame that I had not the heart to shoot them, in their second season they were still more confiding, and most of them, unaccountably preserved from the foxes, are still with us. One of the ducks, with anything up to four passionate drakes in close attendance, has taken to using the swimming-pool in the evenings, and elements of the garrison are continually being committed to clamorous and inconvenient sorties in attempts to break her of this undesirable habit. She appears rather to enjoy this Cold War.

I think I have covered most of the major points which have arisen during the past seven years from my ownership of a swimming-pool, but it is perhaps worth mentioning that a pool of the primitive type I have described costs virtually nothing to maintain. It is true that 70,000 gallons of water at 3s. 3d. a thousand gallons works out at over £10 a year; but the nearest decent bathing place (admission 2s.) is ten miles from my house, and you don't have to have many hot days in a summer before you have spent £10 taking three children and their friends to swim in a crowded reach of the river.

ULCERS FOR ALL

I was greatly struck by a full-page advertisement which appeared in last week's *Spectator*, and doubtless also in other periodicals which, for better or for worse, I fail to scan. It heralded a series of articles which the *Daily Herald* is publishing this week under the title of "Don't be Afraid of the Future!"

I suppose there is no great harm in our being told that fear of the future is superfluous; but I vaguely resent the main implication of this announcement. It is, surely, that such a fear is widespread and needs allaying. To whistle in the dark is foolish but natural; to whistle in the sunlight is unbecoming. Had any of our political leaders been so ill-advised as to coin this slogan at the time of Dunkirk—when the future held nothing but fears—he would have met with ridicule and contempt, and this slogan would have become a music-hall joke overnight. Today its soppy message is less obviously out of tune with the mood of the nation; but to suggest (as the author of the *Daily Herald* article does) that because of the frightful state of insecurity in which we live "fear is chasing fear round the minds of millions" is to depict a community not readily recognisable to its members.

"The natives," Mr. Drew Middleton cabled to the *New York Times* from London on the same day that these words appeared, "are in an odd mood." His lighthearted but percipient analysis of this mood included no reference to the haggard forebodings discernible on all sides from Transport House; and there are few closer observers of the English scene.

The word "slogan" started life as sluagh-gairm, which means a war-cry in Gaelic, but since then, as the dictionary admits, it has come down in the world, via "party cry, watchword, motto," to "short catchy phrase used in advertising." Admittedly the *Daily Herald* needs all the advertisement it can get. But the methods by which their ingenious manufacturers peddle patent medicines and cures for baldness are not really congruous to the enunciation of political doctrine; and "Don't be Afraid of the Future" echoes unmistakably the Before-It-Is-Too-Late, Even-Your-Best-Friends-Won't-Tell-You parrot cries which urge us to take precautions against dizziness, dandruff and body odour.

A lot of people worry, whatever the state of their own or the nation's destinies. Some have cruel cause to worry; some have cause to worry but do not do so; some would worry if you gave them perfect health, unlimited wealth and round-the-clock police protection; some enjoy worrying. But on the whole the British are not the worrying kind. They are not, indeed, fatalistic. They do not say "Never mind" as often as the Russians say "*Nichevo,*" nor "It can't be helped" as often as the Chinese say "*Mei yü fa-tzu*"; but if you ask a Briton of the less highly educated classes how he does, the chances are that he will reply, "Might be worse" or even, specifically, "Mustn't grumble."

I therefore deplore as dishonest an attempt (however clumsy) to depict our nation, or a large part of it, as racked with fear of the future. I think it is plain silly to write, as the man in the *Daily Herald* does, of hundreds of thousands of people "struggling against all the odds that a callous and Philistine society can stack against them." The Welfare State may deserve the epithet Philistine; but one would have to be either hysterical or Russian to call it callous.

I can remember some pretty inane political slogans— "Safety First," "Hats Off to France," "Lend to Defend the Right to be Free"—but I really think that "Don't be Afraid of the Future!" must be the wettest offspring of a Highland war-cry we have heard for a long, long time.

ON ACTUALLY WRITING

I AM writing.

Looking over my shoulder, the ghost of my long-dead governess compliments itself on recognising the vestiges of the pothooks she taught me to fashion. I remember those pothooks, the trellis-work on which the authentic letters of the alphabet would one day in a moment of triumph suddenly burgeon, as loyal heraldry proclaims itself, sizzling and incandescent, against the night sky on the Fourth of June.

The pothooks were formal, delicate, drooping growths, like tropic ferns in a conservatory. It is clever of my governess's ghost to recognise them after all these years. From my nib the calligraphy which she implanted in me now goes into action like a squadron of cavalry emerging from a defile upon some reckless charge. The vowels seem to bury their faces in the manes of the striding and half-frantic consonants. A full stop is a spent cannon-ball, a paragraph a sunken road; neither checks, as both usefully could, the doomed and ineffective onrush of my scrawl.

"Onrush" may have given the impression that I write very fast. It is, alas, a misleading impression! When I think of some words to write, I put them down as quickly as I possibly can; then I stop, and gaze vacantly out of the window at the wheat, and the woods beyond the wheat, and the blue spine of an alien and far-distant county showing above the woods.

"It must," visitors quite often opine, "be a wonderful place to write in. So peaceful." Peaceful! I survey a battlefield. It is true that the belligerents are not in action all the time and that most of the fighting takes place out of sight; but aggression is continuously afoot. That jay, whose lolloping, deceptively abstracted flight takes him across my wide arc of vision, breaks his journey at the ash tree in midfield. Nothing wrong with that. But why is he now slowly and silently descending the tree, hopping down from one branch to the next with his head (as I can see through field-glasses) cocked on one side? Is *that* where the partridge's nest is, in the long grass underneath the ash?

The sound of contented munching below my window draws attention to the fact that one of the ponies has got into the garden and is tucking into the herbaceous border. I rise to my feet, the two dogs leap to theirs, the ghost of my governess vanishes.

I am not writing any longer.

I am much impressed by the genuine curiosity which ordinary, decent people seem to feel about what may be called the manual side of authorship. I noticed at an early stage of my literary career that far the commonest question I had to answer about my works was how I got them on to paper in the first place. "Do you actually write it all down yourself," people used to ask, "with a pen or a pencil? Or do you use a typewriter? Perhaps you dictate everything? Which do you think is the *best* way?"

At first I supposed this catechism to imply a latent incredulity, a reluctance to believe that a person like myself was capable of literary composition. I assumed that the questions were like those addressed to a child who claims to have performed some improbable though not impossible feat; their purpose was to try—tactfully and without a premature display of scepticism—to establish whether or not I could give a convincing account of how I had done what I was alleged to have done.

But I soon learned, from more respectable authors, that this itch to know how writers perform the act of writing is very widespread among the reading public: in whom, if I may say so, it seems to me to betray an enlightened spirit of inquiry.

There must exist in the literary world men and women who show a proper regard for the tools of their trade, who clean their typewriter after using it as automatically as one cleans one's gun, who would no more write with an obsolete fountain-pen than an up-to-date photographer would rely on a Brownie. Pencil-sharpeners, rubber bands and other accessories are symmetrically arrayed upon their tidy desks. They know to the nearest dozen how many words they will write upon a page. They take the quiet pride which craftsmen should in selecting and maintaining their equipment.

I have, however, the impression that these enviable individuals represent only a small minority of the profession to which they belong. Perhaps because writing is such an intolerably difficult and uncertain business, most writers overlook the part (which appears to them negligible) that technology might play in making it easier. They cling obstinately to techniques, implements and materials which they adopted, years ago, more or less by accident. Those whose writing is legible only with difficulty take no pains to improve it, but accept, as though they were penalties ordained by Providence, the handicaps thus imposed on their secretaries and the extra time they themselves have to spend correcting typescripts. Those who once formed the habit of sharpening pencils with an old razor-blade continue to do so till the end of their lives, as though they were castaways upon some ill-provided desert island.

Most writers, I am sure, would never dream of pursuing a hobby in the feckless, slovenly way in which, on the material side, we follow our professions. If I owned a small boat I should keep it in far more shipshape order than I keep my desk. I would never try to catch a salmon with a reel that constantly jammed and a worn-out line; what on earth makes me think that I may write a masterpiece on a typewriter purchased nineteen years ago in Hong Kong, clogged with fluff and given to harbouring woodlice? As for my fountain-pen——

But I must lay my fountain-pen aside. Two fallow deer have appeared in the far end of the wheat and must be extruded. Something tells me that, even if I do get a decent typewriter, my output will not materially improve until I brick up this damned window.

MAGNIFIQUE

I AM against the employment of words which have no meaning at all. Many such are in common use, but to some must be granted a form of dramatic or poetic licence. It would, for instance, be hard on orators to require them to construe all their utterances. The lives of public men, already scarcely supportable, would be even more gruelling if they could not proclaim "Siam is a bastion of democracy" without being asked to explain (using one side of the paper only) exactly what they meant.

In orators, leader-writers, bishops and others who use words as missiles of mass-destruction a certain lack of precision is by custom permissible; the lexicographers label it "fig.," for figurative. When whoever it was enriched our national idiom by asserting that the privileged classes were "grinding the faces of the poor," nobody inquired of him how this inhuman but difficult process was carried out. The orator enjoys the same sort of immunity from cross-examination on matters of detail which used to prevent one's nanny from being challenged when she said, in a minatory tone, that she knew many a little boy roaming the streets of London who would be only too glad to finish up one's spinach.

The sky above us is so criss-crossed with vapour-trails of rodomantade, jargon, dialectic, sales-talk and other forms of etymological mumbo-jumbo that we have come to accept a situation in which many of the most cogent-sounding phrases are about as full of meaning as an addled egg is of meat. When politicians and generals talk about the "new, streamlined infantry division" we give them credit for *wanting* the words to mean something, perhaps for a moment we half-share their vision of an entirely novel type of field formation, as lean and agile as a lizard. Only if we stop to think do we realise that by slightly reducing the number of men and vehicles in a division you do not make it streamlined (whatever that may be); you merely make it smaller.

Only the more costive type of purist would pick a serious quarrel with those semi-graphic, semi-pretentious phrases, those sheep in sheep's clothing, which the planners have introduced into our vocabulary. If it makes people happier to say "The working party has produced a blueprint" instead of "The committee has made a plan," let them say it; it does no more harm than the Meteorological Office's new habit of talking about "the general weather situation" when it means "the weather."

But here and there, out-topping the rank jungle of our usage, stands an immemorial tree whose trunk, without anyone suspecting it, has been hollowed by decay. The word is not obsolete, has not been compromised by misuse, still *seems* to have its pristine vigour and validity; yet it describes something which has so altered its character as to cause doubt whether it exists at all. One such word is "strategy."

Strategy, the dictionary says, is "generalship, the art of war (lit. and fig.); management of an army or armies in a campaign, art of so moving or disposing troops or ships as to impose on the enemy the place and time and conditions preferred by oneself (cf. TACTICS)"; and strategic means "of, dictated by, serving the ends of, strategy."

The noun and its adjective are still widely used; they retain the authoritative, not to say portentous, overtones to which, in the slow-moving wars of Alexander the Great and Napoleon, they were entitled. But do they actually *mean* anything today? Neither an intercontinental bombardment programme nor the technical arrangements which will make it possible come within the scope of the dictionary's definitions. When the Government reveals that it is considering the establishment of a "strategic base" in East Africa, has it in fact excogitated a strategy of which such a base would serve the ends, or is it merely looking for a non-controversial site on which to dump a large quantity of barbed wire?

There is a strong, perhaps an overwhelming, case to be made out for stationing in Western Europe a small British force of 77,000 officers and men; but that case could only be said to rest on strategic grounds if strategy also meant "the art of so disposing troops as to ensure

142

their certain defeat in the opening phase of the only foreseeable military operation by the land forces of the enemy."

War is, regrettably, the only form of corporate enterprise to which a State devotes the whole of its energies. Religion, agriculture and (latterly) industry have been the province of specialist though often large minorities. It has been only to war that communities in their entirety have, with however much reluctance, dedicated themselves.

It is perhaps for this reason that the essential vocabulary of war has retained, beneath endless accretions, a certain sacrosanctity. When a staff officer refers in a written appreciation to the enemy (however numerous) as "he," he is not perpetuating an affectation; he is crystallising the experience of *homo sapiens* in innumerable wars. For all armies, and perhaps still more all navies, have hitherto known instinctively that the true adversary is "he" and not "they"; that on the other side of the hill or the ocean there was, somewhere, a man who took decisions which he hoped would enable him to impose his will on their will and to defeat them. He was not, perhaps, a very personal figment to the fighting men; but by their commanders, though he was sometimes under- and sometimes over-rated, he was never forgotten.

He was a strategist; so was his opponent. Either could lose or win a war or a campaign. Now both have been superseded. The enemy is still "he," we no doubt are still "he" to him. But he is no longer a strategist; he is an individual who pushes a button and hopes for the best.

Either we need a new word to describe him, or the editors of the *Oxford English Dictionary* must turn up "strategy," slip into something loose, and give themselves up to an agonising reappraisal.

A HALT AT MTSENSK

Four hundred and eighty miles is quite far enough to drive in a day, and when we reached Mtsensk on our way back to Moscow we were both tired.

The morning had been hot and glaring, but in the afternoon we ran into a storm of tropical intensity. The downpour of rain and hail had more bite, more venom than real tropical storms have. The great empty land was darkened. The volume of water hitting the wind-screen was such that the whirring wipers made no difference. Traffic came to a standstill; lorries and carts pulled off the highway on to the treeless verge and awaited better things. Only the Zephyr, with lights blazing, continued to carve a bow-wave out of the scarcely visible road. Long, melodramatic shafts of lightning snaked down the blackness ahead. Thunder cannonaded. From the back of the car where our inter-preter huddled there seemed to come faintly (but I may be wronging Vladimir) an intermittent mewing.

The rearguards of this storm still rumbled round us when we reached Mtsensk. We had noted on our journey south that the main part of the town lay off the highway, to the east. There were cupolas and spires; the place, seen from a distance, had a less functional and regi-mented air than most townships in that part of Russia. For some reason we had looked forward to Mtsensk.

By the time we got there we would have looked for-ward to Slough. We had left Zaporozhe at seven o'clock, which was too early to get a cup of tea in the hotel (where a lady of—for Russia—startling beauty was found dossed down on a sofa in the corridor outside our room). We had breakfasted at the Russian equivalent of a Good Pull-up for Carmen after three hours' driving: a friendly, rather Hogarthian place of which our interpreter fought shy while we fended for ourselves. For luncheon we had eaten some dubious sandwiches and drunk boiling mineral water out of the boot. It was on creature comforts that our minds were fixed when we drove into the environs of Mtsensk.

As we did so, an ominous sight met our eyes: a road-sign with "To the Hotel: 5 Kms." on it.

"Did you see that?" asked Duff. In such a tone might some early settler in a savage land have pointed out to his companion the still-warm embers of a head-hunters' camp fire on the trail leading back to his homestead. I nodded gravely.

In most Russian towns—as, no doubt, in Slough—the traveller finds his way to the principal hotel without assistance from the highway authorities. Only once before had we seen signs saying "To the Hotel." Then they had led us to an establishment erected on the road-side by the Ministry which makes the roads. Blind, un-thinking fools that we were, it had never occurred to us that there might be another of these ghastly places. But after five kilometres there was.

Lenin and Stalin, painted silver, stood sentinel outside an exact replica of the chalet-type barrack we had left behind in the Ukraine a week earlier. An exact replica? Not quite.

"Yes, yes," muttered Vladimir, skipping with alacrity into Fort Zinderneuf. "Certainly you will be able to get a bath. I will tell them to send the porter for our luggage."

Porters, or anyhow doorkeepers, do exist in ordinary Russian hotels. They are old men with what I can only describe as uncontemporary faces. Their fathers, I sup-pose, were serfs, for serfdom was abolished less than a century ago, yet their features have—against the background of two younger and freer generations—an almost aristocratic cast. They may be oafs, but they do not look oafish. "I fought in three wars," they will tell you (for they count the Civil War, reasonably enough, as a third). "I have had a hard life." Their faces express the same capacity for loyalty, the same vague bemusement, the same infinite goodwill that you see in a Labrador who knows his day is past and who is left at home with Nanny and the children on shooting days.

We knew better than to expect one of these nice old men at Mtsensk. We unloaded the luggage and carried it in. Vladimir met us.

"I am sorry," he said. "I have misinformed you. There is no bath."

Our room was identical with the room we had stayed in farther south. A small wireless set in one corner muttered to itself. Duff, who is powerfully built, forced the double windows open. The door, which had possibly had no first-hand experience of the elements since the place was built six years ago, blew open. We shut it. It blew open again. We locked it.

"I'm going to wash," said Duff.

But when he turned the key nothing happened. After a lot of rattling a rescue squad came and let us out. The mineral water which we had ordered on arrival turned up after twenty minutes. I had a whisky and soda while Duff washed.

I took his place at the tap in the lavatory along the corridor. A trickle of water came out of it, then dried up altogether. Several members of the staff assembled and gazed at the tap. They reached the conclusion that the water supply had failed.

Outside the rain poured down. A fountain in front of the hotel played like mad. I found a jug of drinking

146

water and washed in that. A plumber arrived, a very sad man. The sound of hammering echoed down the corridor.

Tripping over the suitcase with which we had wedged the door, Vladimir entered to announce that there was no restaurant but a meal would be served in our room. It would be ready in an hour and a half.

For the first time in my life I actively wished I were in Slough.

ON BEING MIDDLE-AGED

I WAS once required to write an essay on Browning's idiotic slogan:

> Grow old along with me;
> The best is yet to be.

I cannot, mercifully, remember what I wrote, but I do remember thinking that it was a silly subject to have to write about when you were seventeen.

At seventeen both sexes wish to appear—and indeed, if it could only be arranged, to be—older than they are. Though they are mostly a good deal less mature than they suppose themselves, they possess one ideal attribute of old age which they are certain to lose in later life and which they are not certain to recapture in their eighties. They are tolerant of their juniors.

Their own childhood they see in a clear perspective, as something sloughed off and mildly ridiculous. It has for them no golden, irrecoverable aura; their minds do not hark wistfully back to its triumphs, and on its failures only frivolous post-mortems are held. They watch without jealousy the lower age groups clambering over the kindergarten obstacles which they painfully surmounted ten long years ago. They may try to help, but they do not try to reform; they may criticise, but they do not disapprove. Their attitude is that of a male dog to his puppies: friendly, long-suffering, but not involved. They regard most small children as a nuisance; but they do not discern in them all a threat, or a challenge, or a cause for serious misgivings.

At seventeen one's elders outnumber one's juniors, and one is just beginning to discover them. Although in general it is still seen as a menace, the dread battle-array of the grown-ups no longer presents a monolithic phalanx. Godfathers and gamekeepers and perhaps even schoolmasters, old fishermen and dashing cousins of twenty-seven who ten years ago had seemed to belong to another era—figures like these keep deserting across the no-man's land between youth and age, throwing off the disguise of enemy or hero and turning out to be friends, people whose society one can enjoy on almost equal terms.

But the concept of growing old is as far beyond our grasp at seventeen as the concept of growing up was at seven, when boring people often asked us what we were going to do when we had completed this mysterious but dull process. Old age was a subject which may well have interested the master who set me the essay more than thirty years ago; but for me it was beyond apprehension, almost beyond surmise.

If he had garbled Browning's lines into

> Grow old on Mars with me:
> The best is yet to be

everybody concerned would have had a better run for their money; for although we were not obsessed with Space, H. G. Wells and Edgar Rice Burroughs, who besides creating Tarzan pioneered in space-fiction, had given us a grounding into its possibilities. At seventeen any boy can write with feeling, and even with vision of a sort, about life on another planet; none can put himself in the slippers of a septuagenarian or even imagine what it is like to be fifty.

A man of fifty is the same age, roughly, as a twelve-year-old horse or a seven-year-old dog; what—in my experience—he never seems to be is the same age as any other man of fifty. I do not mean by this that middle-aged men are dishonest or evasive about their ages, as middle-aged women sometimes are. They become, indeed, most precise and meticulous in these matters.

"George must be fifty-three at least. Probably fifty-four. He went down at the end of my first year, and I'm fifty-one."

"Fifty-one? I thought you were younger than me."

"No, no, old boy. Birthday last month."

Such colloquies are characterised by an almost nanny-like regard for chronological exactitude.

It is but natural that some men of fifty should look older than their contemporaries, and vice versa. Some have grey hair, or practically no hair at all; some have become very fat, others have a shrunken, desiccated air. Health, heredity and habits of life have contributed to these external contrasts. More interesting, to me, are the widely differing attitudes which we adopt towards the inescapable fact that we are middle-aged.

Some, if they have not capitulated to Time, seem to be carrying out a planned withdrawal. Phrases like "got to be careful these days" are often on their lips. They give up things like brandy and beagling with a prudent and rather self-righteous alacrity. In the country they armour themselves against the wind and the rain with an intricate assortment of chill-proof and impermeable garments. They go to bed early and eat little pills with their breakfast.

Then there are those who seem to be engaged on a

rearguard action against senescence. They walk home from the office or the station, do exercises, diet themselves and take other temperate measures designed to keep time at bay. I admire these men, especially when they do not boast (as they are apt to do) about the disciplines to which they subject themselves.

Finally—though, of course, there are many intermediate gradations—there are the men (it is a moot point whether they should be described as reckless or feckless) who at fifty go on playing squash, riding in point-to-points, getting soaked to the skin, drinking liberal quantities of spirits and otherwise tempting Providence. Put one of these alongside the "got-to-be-careful-these-days" man and you would find it hard to believe that they were the same age, or to guess which will be first into a bath-chair.

But whatever line we take, whatever posture we strike, whether our attitude to Time is over-deferential or over-cavalier, all men of fifty have in my belief one thing in common: we are all extremely lucky, after half a century, to be alive and—more or less—sane.

SLIM VOLUME

Sequels are almost always disappointing. When I compare 640989 with 526239, or indeed with any of the intervening editions of this indispensable publication, I am aware of a falling off. The format is the same; the frontispiece, though slightly different, is as repellent as it was in 1925; and the slim volume is no slimmer. It still says on the flyleaf: "This Passport contains 32 pages"; and it still adds, lest some clueless Kalmuck cannot understand English: "*Ce passeport contient 32 pages.*" This, I suppose, is a precaution against the bearer either tearing out a compromising page ("The accused, m'lud, maintains that he was never in Siam. I have here . . .") or alternatively inserting a couple of extra ones covered with forged visas.

I note with approval that the practice of printing Passport with a capital and *passeport* without one is still adhered to. The nuance, a subtle one, is clearly intended to remind foreigners that my passport is a British official document, on which the French language, though employed for convenience and as matter of condescension, has a subordinate status.

Of the various world-trends which reveal themselves to a textual critic of successive editions the most striking is the decline of the personality-cult among British Foreign Secretaries. The first of these dignitaries to request - and - require - all-those - whom-it-may-concern-to-allow-the-bearer-to-pass-freely-without-let-or-hindrance-and-to afford - him - every - assistance - and - protection - of - which-he-may-stand-in-need began, "We, George Nathaniel, Marquess Curzon of Kedleston, Earl of Kedleston, Viscount Scarsdale, Baron Ravensdale, Knight of the Most Noble Order of the Garter, Knight Grand Commander, . . ." and so on, until the catalogue of his honours ended, on a note of petulant satiety, with "etc. etc. etc." Below the preamble appeared his coat of arms and a facsimile of his signature.

Seven years later Sir John Allsebrook Simon was still addressing the foreigners in the first person plural. His "etc. etc. etc." has a hint of ostentation, perhaps even of imposture, about it, but his coat of arms includes a bird which looks to me like a razorbill, thus adding an agreeable touch of Lewis Carroll to the document.

What do we find when we turn to 640989? A drab anonymity. No signature, no heraldry. Merely, printed on a coloured background suggestive of a petrol coupon,

"Her Britannic Majesty's Principal Secretary of State for Foreign Affairs requests and requires. . . ." Anyone can see that we have come down in the world.

This is borne out by much other evidence. An American visa issued (without any nonsense about fingerprints) in 1929 bears the legend, "Fee $10 = £2 1s. 8d."; in those days there was no need for the last two pages to be devoted to the sordid and parsimonious particulars of "Foreign Exchange for Travelling Expenses." What has become of J. P. Thompson, Chief Commissioner, Delhi, who in 1931 with the aid of a single rubber stamp could blithely scrawl across one page, "Also valid for Persia, Iraq, Syria, Turkey, Bulgaria, Yugo Slavia"? Where nowadays will you find a Sanders whose writ runs so far down the river?

Turn, for a sorry contrast, to 640989, the latest edition. No fewer than nine of its thirty-two pages are taken up by large purple visas issued by the Foreign Office authorising me to enter the petty sheikdoms along the Trucial Coast. In the old days it was the foreigners whom we blamed for wasting the space in our passports with huge, blurred, meaningless stencils and gawdy stamps. "We, George Nathaniel," would never have needed nine pages of my passport to give me the run of Ras-al-Khaimal, Umm-al-Qaiwain and the rest of these obscure sand dunes (which, incidentally, I never went to in the end).

All editions carry on the back page the statement that "this passport is a valuable document." Only the latest finds it necessary to add that it is "the property of Her Majesty's Government and may be withdrawn at any time." Here again we get a glimpse of a world-trend, a reminder that we have passed into an age where subversion, defection and treachery are contingencies which cannot be left out of account.

Thumbing through the 170 pages which span the thirty-two years between Lord Curzon's coat of arms and Mr. Selwyn Lloyd's petrol coupon, between the bun-faced boy of the first frontispiece and the cornered dope-fiend of the last, I am impressed by the prodigious and almost worldwide waste of effort for which my passport has been responsible. Hundreds of conscientious men have scrutinised it, stamped it and appended their signatures. Chinamen and Turks, Guatemalans and Poles and Britons have recorded its particulars. Behind them, unseen, in the *Oficina de Pasaportes* or the *Yamen* of the Provincial Government or the Immigration Office, clerks have filed these particulars; and behind the clerks dour boobies in the secret police have, in countries like Russia and Japan, made further annotations. Men have got up early in the morning or stayed up late at night in order to make hieroglyphic marks on the stiff little pages.

I myself, the bearer of this valuable document which though I have paid for it does not belong to me, have spent hours standing in queues, bustling from consulate to consulate, waiting in anterooms, presenting certificates of inoculation, filling up forms. In the pursuit of exotic visas I have blustered, pleaded, if necessary lied. So far from conferring immunity from lets and hindrances, my passport has involved me in a wide variety of them.

Not a minute, not a second of time passes in which, all over the world, fretting travellers are not presenting their passports to bored officials. Never was so vast and cumbersome a net spread to catch so few aberrant fish; but all fish, however lawful their occasions, have to go through it. The passport system must surely represent the purest, if not the biggest, diversion of effort which *homo sapiens* has imposed upon himself.

WHY YOU NO THUMPA DA CHEST?

It is believed widely, and nowhere more firmly than in these islands, that the British are a modest race, averse from boasting and prone to understatement; in this they are held to differ from the Americans, the citizens of Eire and all save the more congenitally inscrutable types of foreigner. I suppose this is broadly speaking true: but it cannot always have been true, or we should never have had Hotspur and Falstaff and the countless other bigmouths who recur throughout our literature. How did we lose the habit? Why nowadays do we boast so rarely, and with so little true flamboyance? Why do we not thump our chests and rant?

The short answer is that we are more self-conscious than we used to be. The inhibitions thus induced are strengthened by a vague feeling, inculcated in all classes at school if from no other source, that boasting is bad form; compulsory education must have been, at the least, a member of the firing squad that did away with braggadocio. Fifty years ago the public schoolboy who made a century for his First XI restrained his natural impulse to boast (for it is after all a very natural impulse) because he knew that boasting was not "the done thing." But I suspect that a young ploughman of the same period, after making a century for his village, probably did boast a bit in the pub that evening, and as long as he didn't overdo it was thought none the worse of. Today he too would mumblingly dismiss his innings as a fluke.

But the truth is that boasting is only one method of showing off. This method has, owing to certain traits in their character, become unfashionable and indeed almost tabu among the British; they are not however thereby debarred from showing off in other, more subtle, but not less effective ways. The man who insists that his century was a fluke and reminds you that he was dropped in the gully when he had made twenty-four is not less surely laying a claim to your approbation than the braggart is. Both employ diametrically opposite techniques, but their objectives are not really very different.

This devious approach to self-glorification is paralleled by a certain eccentricity in our choice of things to boast about. No bishop (I feel sure I am right in saying) ever boasts about being a bishop, though his wife may give herself airs; but if he won, say, a literary competition in the *Spectator* under a *nom de guerre* he might easily be tempted to boast about that.

Let us suppose that he yields to the temptation, and examine the consequences; for they will illustrate the extraordinary *difficulty* of boasting under the elaborate British conventions. Remark first that he is on a relatively easy wicket, for the *Spectator*—or so I have always understood—is widely read among the clergy, and the problem of bringing the conversation round to the field in which the bishop has excelled will not loom so large for him as it would if he had got a right and left at woodcock or achieved some other abstruse but uncultured distinction.

So the odds are in his favour. Sooner or later his casual opening gambit ("Do you ever see the *Spectator* these days?") is bound to give him the conversational toe-hold he requires. Later, probably, rather than sooner—for people when asked if they read a weekly paper seldom limit their reply to "Yes" but launch into a considered analysis of its demerits and of their own confessedly inadequate reasons for not having cancelled their subscription—the bishop will have an opportunity of making, as infantrymen say, his next bound and getting on to the competitions.

Here he must at all costs avoid the sort of direct question which may elicit a "Never look at them, I'm afraid" and thus put the ball irretrievably out of court. He yearns for the other man (I see him, now, as a rather plump geodeticist eating cold brawn and Russian salad at one of the window tables in the Athenæum) to give the Tempter a walkover, to say: "Oh, rather. I thought last week's particularly amusing. I wonder who 'Bimbo' can be?" But these golden opportunities of making a boast without actually boasting are commoner in literature than in life. The chances that the bishop will in the end be able to trot out his small, disarming triumph are still, if he is a man of sensibility, only about evens.

You cannot boast, any more than you can act, without an audience. The braggart aims at mass-hypnosis: he doesn't mind who hears. The British line-shooter doesn't mind how many gather, silently, to listen as he warms to his theme; but his quest for an initial audience is conducted on selective and relatively humane lines.

This does not, of course, apply to a female audience; for the British, like the rest of mankind, work on the assumption that it is one of the privileges of the weaker sex to act as a sort of wastepaper-basket for their reminiscences. The ladies, demons for punishment, have for one reason or another never taken any effective action to destroy this world-wide illusion. This is really just as well, for it pre-conditions them to tolerate, in the persons of their children, the only braggarts who often do need to be taken seriously.

The muted, half-apologetic note in British braggadocio can be detected even when we boast, vicariously, about the achievements of our dogs and our horses. Pride becomes, I think, more explicit when we show off our gardens; and—perhaps because they are impersonal things—we do not scruple to extol labour-saving gadgets which we have newly acquired in terms only less fulsome than those employed by the manufacturer.

We like having our boasting done for us. Our wives or our husbands, our parents or our friends, should all (when there is anything to boast about) be dedicated to this duty; but if we catch them discharging it we must, by an unwritten law, disown and ridicule their efforts. Here it is not a question of pointing out that we were dropped in the gully when we had made twenty-four; we must insist that we never made a century at all.

My grandmother, when I and my three brothers were at school, was indefatigable in this rather thankless role of PRO. The legend ran that, when one brother became Victor Ludorum at Eton, she approached a group of strangers in a Riviera hotel and, thumping a folded copy of *The Times* as though it were a tambourine, cried: "Look! My grandson is Victor Ludendorff!"

Staunch to the national tradition, we retaliated by teasing her. "Dear Granny" (I once wrote),

> I know you will be pleased to hear, after Ian's success as Victor Ludendorff, that I have won the Duke of Wellington's Knitting Prize, while Richard, young though he is, came second in a newt-catching competition at Datchet which was open to *the whole school*. The dear little fellow is still looking rather pale with strain. . . .

Baseless though they were, I wish I could believe that these claims were the nearest I have ever come to braggadocio.

THE SPINACH-SPIES OF
PORTLAND PLACE

"I want some meat."

"Yes, sir," said the butcher. I could see that he expected me to particularise. His small shop was festooned with meat. It would have been better to have been more specific in the first place.

I asked for cutlets. From a planning point of view the cutlet is an easy unit to deal with. Start dabbling in technicalities like tenderloins and saddles and briskets and you may find yourself bulk-purchasing and finish up with enough food for a fortnight.

"Family away?" asked the butcher's wife in a faintly compassionate tone while her husband got to work with his chopper.

"Yes," I said.

Because two Labradors normally travel in my car, I always put the meat in the boot. I then forget all about it and have spaghetti for luncheon because Inge, the Danish cook, assumes that I have omitted to order any meat. I thus prove to be an economical housekeeper.

I am however overwhelmed by a sense of my inadequacy in this role when I listen to *Shopping List*, a five-minute programme which the BBC puts out twice a week at 8.15 a.m. It consists of what staff officers would call a sitrep on food, and is read by the announcer. It seems to have superseded a similar programme called *Shopping Flash*. This was read, in rotation, by a small team of rather effusive ladies; it was chatty and personal ("there's more than a hint of autumn round the corner when you find apples tumbling into season"). I always switched it off.

The new programme, on the other hand, exerts a curious fascination on me. This is partly because of announcer-participation. When I hear those grave, mellifluous, demi-official tones exhorting us "when choosing cucumbers, look to see they are firm," or suggesting that "if your fishmonger sells double fillets of haddock, these will probably be cheaper per pound than the single fillets," I become sharply aware of what a many-faceted business one man's life can be. I find something piquant in the fact that the voice which ten minutes ago was apprising us of portentous events, telling us of disasters and detonations and Mr. Dulles, is now, in exactly the same well-modulated accents, revealing that "cauliflowers have had particular recommendation in the Glasgow area." There is a faint but unmistakable note of parody about the whole thing which I like very much.

Brief and impersonal though it is, the transmission opens up—or, rather, affords a glimpse of—a new, an unfamiliar, a challenging world. It is a world in which I myself would soon get lost. "Flake," said the BBC on August 9, "should be cheaper than it has been recently." I do not know what flake is.* Textual evidence suggests that it is some sort of fish, but were I to inquire the price of a pound of it (or should it be a pound of *them*? Perhaps flake are tiny little creatures, like whitebait) how could I possibly tell whether the price quoted was lower than it had been recently? I should be a mere gull, at the mercy of an unscrupulous fishmonger.

"Seventeen and six?" I would quaver. "Isn't that rather a *lot* for a pound? The BBC said——"

"Seventeen and six a lot for a pound of *flake*!" the

* The BBC may have said "hake"; but the word appears, *passim*, as "flake" in the scripts which my ubiquitous agents have procured for me.

fishmonger would roar indignantly. "Come, come, sir! You'll be telling me I don't know my own business next!"

And I would pay up, blushing and muttering apologies. A great pale hunk of fish would join the spare wheel and the grouse-feathers in the oubliette.

I immensely admire the assurance with which the BBC picks its way, unerring and authoritative, about this strange, still-life, cornucopian world, judiciously quizzing the saithe and the persimmons, the bilberries and the chicken halibut (is this an old trade name for flying fish?). How do they do it? What are their sources of information?

You have only to listen to the stuff they transmit to realise that its collation and assessment must be the work of an intelligence service, and a highly organised one at that. However casually the announcer may make them, statements like "Dover soles are recommended, and there is *some good quality line-caught halibut*" reflect an advanced standard of training among the BBC's food-spies. As, turning up their coat collars, they pause to light an unobtrusive cigarette in front of the fishmonger's slab, can they tell by the expression on the halibut's lifeless face that it was caught on a line and not in a net? I suppose they must be able to.

"In several areas smal Queen pineapples are inexpensive." What a lot of travelling they must do to obtain even so trivial an item of intelligence! And, if it comes to that, what a lot of eating, or at least nibbling! "The straight, perfectly formed beans are more expensive, but the flavouring of *all* is good." My italics, but they miss nothing. "There are some globe artichokes in the Bristol area. . . . Some cherries are split. . . . Prawns are in first-class condition. . . . Shoppers are advised to look for filleted codling."

It is bootless and might be indiscreet to speculate too

160

closely about the methods by which the BBC has built up this nation-wide spy-ring; but no one can listen to its terse, oracular reports without feeling admiration for the anonymous men and women who have spent the previous day scurrying from counter to counter, prodding flounders, pinching pears, counting radishes and noting the price of gammon.

Are there ever any repercussions? I have noticed, for instance, that cheese is never mentioned. No doubt there is some good reason for this, but has no irate deputation from the National Association of Cheesemakers ever demanded to know what it is? And is the BBC being fair to fishmongers when it gives the public advice on how to get a bargain in haddock?

Finally, how on earth did shoppers *manage* in the days before wireless, when they could not listen for five minutes twice a week to an urbane voice telling them that "Pickled brisket is a little dearer than the forequarter flank"? This small, beneficent BBC programme supplies —to borrow a diagnosis applied over several decades by the great Beachcomber to the pullulating amenities of our society—proof (if proof were needed) that we are not living in the Middle Ages.

THE CAT IS ON THE MAT

Last night in a place where from time to time I go for a drink a big, fat man with a scowl on his face stalks up to me and says:

"Most of the words you use in those things you write each week are far too *long*. I do not like long words; lots of us round here do not like them. We do not know what some of them mean, or at least we are not sure if we do. They give us a pain in the neck. What the hell is wrong with short words? Why do you not use more of them? It may be that you think it is smart to write the way you do. Well, I and my pals do not share that view. See?"

I turn pale. "Do you mean," I ask him, "that you wish me to change my style?"

"I mean just that," he says. He has a hard, cold eye like a snake. "Lay off the long words from now on. Stick to short ones."

"How short do they have to be?" I bleat.

"As short as they come!" he snaps.

"Do you mean," I gasp, "that all the words I use have got to be mon——"

He jumps down my throat. "There you go!" he shouts. "Can you not leave long words out of it? You tried to sneak one in then, did you not? You had best watch your step!" And he lets fly a foul oath which I cannot print here as one of the words in it is a non-mon.

Meek as an eft, I say that I will do my best.

I am sure it will not be hard to do the task I have been set. Just now, it is true, I feel like one who tries to walk on stilts in deep sand; but that is not to say that I will not soon get the knack and that a great spate of Eng. Lit. (*verb. sap.* in this case) will start to flow from my pen.

So far the worst snag seems to be the choice of a theme. When we start to learn to write we are taught to use none save *les mots les plus courts,* as the French say; and since this is so you might think that to write in this way is kid stuff and does not call for much *nous.*

You can take it from me that this is not the case. The world in which we live is far from rich in the sort of theme on which even a glib old hack like me can write the best part of a page of prose in words of not more than one—well, you know what I mean: in mons.

162

Still, it has got to be done. I have set my hand to the plough, and I do not mean to shirk or scamp the job. I could, of course, just write "The cat is on the mat" and a lot more stuff like that and go on and on and on, though it made no sense at all, till I had done my stint. But I scorn to stoop to such a low dodge. It would bore you stiff, and it might rouse the ire of the Ed. and lead him to think twice ere he paid me the small fee which helps to keep the wolf from my door.

What does make me sad is that so far there are no signs that my Muse is, as one says of a horse, up to the bit. She and I do not seem to have found our length yet. I felt sure that we would get the hang of this new, grape-shot style in a trice and then the sparks would start to fly and the next thing we would know there would be a page and a half in the *Lit. Sup.* on "Strix: The New Look." But some *je ne sais quoi* tells me that things are not going to work out like that, worse luck.

Ah well, *Mei yü fa-tzu,* as the Chinks say; in case you do not know, that means "There is no help for it, there is no way out."

Gosh! That *is* a bright wheeze! I wish I knew a bit more *Chung kuo hwa.* They go in for mons. in a big way; in fact they use naught else. But I dare say that it would look a shade—well, *ping fu,* as Li Po might have put it—were I to drag in a lot of quips and saws from the Far East which were not in the strict sense of the phrase *ad rem.* So I fear that line is no good. Oh dear!

Who was it who wrote:

> "Does the road wind up hill all the way?
> Yes to the v——"

Whew! That was a close shave; and I thought I was on to a cinch. But the bit I quote will show you the way I feel. The strain is, as near as makes no odds, more than

I can stand. And what is it all in aid of? Are all of you like the big fat man and his chums? Do the long words which I am wont, or was wont, to use set your teeth on edge, tax your wits too far, rouse your bile, and bring on *Angst*? And if they do, are these short, small words, these runts of speech which I have been at such pains to round up, more to your taste?

No doubt the long and the short of it is that you do not much care in which style I grind out my tosh. I hope this is so and that next week I may go back to my long words *sans peur* if not *sans* the rest of it. For to be frank this *tour de force* has left me (as in days gone by the French said of an old cab-horse on its last legs) *sur les dents*; and my guess is, it is all hell to a hot-cross bun that things are much the same with you.

YULERY-FOOLERY

When we say, as we quite often do and have done since the dawn of time, that something is not what it used to be, we generally mean that it has shrunk or dwindled. This is not the burden of my complaint against Christmas. In my lifetime Christmas has got bigger, but not better; and at the risk of being thought a curmudgeon I am going to point out some of the flaws (as they seem to me) in contemporary methods of celebrating this festival.

In the first place, Christmas goes on *much too long*. Yule logs start crackling on the covers of the Christmas numbers in November. Decorations in the shops and streets get nearer every year to clashing with the autumnal tints. I know that there are sound reasons for this, but they are basically commercial reasons, and to me there is something synthetic and unattractive in this over-long overture of yulery-foolery. One of the points about a great occasion is that it is an occasion, not an indeterminate tract of time.

Broadcasting is a powerful agent in making Christmas seem to go on and on and on. The BBC is relentlessly seasonable. Its transmitters, like artillery laying down a creeping barrage which will help the poor clueless infantry on to some distant and scarcely attainable objective, start blazing away long before H-hour. Recipes for brandy butter, jokes about turkeys, exhortations to post early, carols, sleigh-bells, excerpts from pantomimes in rehearsal, and a brace of pie-eyed angels on the cover of the *Radio Times*—for days ahead of Christmas itself you can hardly twiddle a knob without getting an earful of artificial snow.

On December 17, for instance, the Home Service offered us a talk on "Christmas in a Four-masted Barque." On the 18th, warming to its work, it broadcast talks on "Christmas in the Bush" and "Preparing for Christmas"; on the 19th we got, or could have got, "Going Home for Christmas" and "Christmas in Benares." On the same day only the fact that it was recorded last September kept all reference to mincepies out of the Third Programme's "Kitchen Problems in Ancient Greece." On the Light Programme regular features like "Women's Hour," "Housewives' Choice" and "Family Favourites" were hock-deep in holly.

None of this does anybody any harm, but it all helps to make us sick of the sound of Christmas before Christmas Day arrives. I think it is a pity. Anticipation ought to be a private pleasure. I can still remember how boring and intrusive I used, as a small boy, to think grown-ups who asked me if I was looking forward to Christmas, or whether I expected that Santa Claus would bring anything for me. It was the mysterious and inviolable parcels accumulating in a forbidden room, the suddenly broken-off conversations of the grown-ups, the general atmosphere of a conspiracy, that made the days leading up to Christmas so exciting. Christmas Day ought to be a climax, a day that goes off like a firework after long and delicious expectation. I am sure it is still a climax for the modern child, but I cannot believe that its status as such is strengthened by all its ingredients being plugged on TV and the wireless for a week or more beforehand.

As I write these anti-seasonable words Christmas is still five days away, yet already well over a hundred Christmas cards have arrived for the members of my household. We sometimes say of a foreign nation that its citizens, though intolerable in the mass, are really quite nice individually. That is how I feel about Christmas cards. I am truly grateful to the people who have sent us these strangely assorted missives—the photograph of their baby or their battleship, the appalling scene of carnage from which their regiment extricated itself in 1777, the reproduction of an old master, the Blankshire in full cry, the robins, angels, turkeys, yule-logs, coaches-and-six, the woodcocks and the greylag geese, the poodles on the lawn of Government House, occasionally even an *avant-garde* version of the ox and the ass and the Object of the Exercise.

But something tells me that it is in the cause of a universally unpopular routine, rather than of goodwill, that the postman has borne through the beechwoods to my house these increments to his normal burden. I believe that a small fortune could be quickly made by anyone who designed a series of agreeable cards, each of which incorporated a deed of covenant binding adult members of the recipient's family not to exchange Christmas cards with the sender for a period of (say) ten years.

These cards, since they could obviously be sent only to

166

close friends, would be regarded as tokens of true esteem and would be highly prized; and although my project, if successful, would adversely affect the interests of the trade, it could hardly fail to benefit those of the community as a whole. Call me a killjoy if you like, but I really cannot see what useful purpose is served by the diversion of effort involved in manufacturing, marketing, addressing, dispatching, delivering and finding temporary lodgement on the mantelpiece for the blizzard of perfunctory and expensive greetings which modern yulery-foolery has imposed on us.

Finally there is the question of parcels. The ultimate purpose of a parcel is to be opened; and although I am sure that many man-hours and scarcely calculable quantities of jute (or whatever string is made of) are saved by doing up parcels with adhesive tape, this ultimate purpose is thereby defeated. A child can worry a modern parcel like a puppy; but it cannot, unaided, get at the contents. I think it is time we stopped wallowing in Christmas and made an effort to preserve its essentials. String is the least of them.

REPORTED SLAIN

Of the four obituary notices I have just been reading three appeared in *The Times* during July, 1900. The fourth was published by the *New York Times* in April, 1940. The only thing which all four have in common is that their subjects, not having been dead when they were printed, were able in due course to read them.

The fourth obituary ("Noted Writer Reported Slain") is my own. It is kept in a drawer full of birth certificates, dogs' pedigrees, unexpended petrol coupons, letters from a long succession of Under-Secretaries of State for War, a *ceadunas tiomana* (which is not a small Minoan urn, a rare seashell or a deadly tropical poison but an Irish driving licence) and obsolete certificates of inoculation against a wide variety of terrible diseases. Most people, I imagine, keep these little caches to which they consign the more *basic* type of personal document under the twin delusions that (*a*) they will be bound to need it one day, and (*b*) they will know where to look for it when they do.

My obituary in the *New York Times* is kindly and even eulogistic, and for that reason dull. But the mere fact of having survived its publication confers a sense of freakish privilege. One feels (quite unjustifiably) that one has played a trick on Fate, that the Grim Reaper has taken an airshot. Without thinking very much about it, I had supposed that a mild, fading, schoolboy glee was the only sentiment likely to be aroused by this particular experience. After reading the three obituaries of fifty-seven years ago I am not so sure.

Their subjects were Sir Claude MacDonald, then Her Majesty's Minister in Peking: Sir Robert Hart, Inspector-General of the Imperial Maritime Customs of China: and Dr. G. E. Morrison, *The Times* Correspondent in Peking. These men were believed, in the light of a false but circumstantial report in the *Daily Mail* of July 15, to have perished in a general massacre of all the foreigners besieged by the Boxers in the Legations.

All three obituaries are, by modern standards, long. They are also quite admirably done—far better, if I may say so without giving offence, than the general run of *The Times* obituaries today. Each, while rehearsing the various stages of its subject's career, evaluates those stages with care and good judgment, so that by the end you have a very exact impression, not only of the man

168

and what he did in the world, but of the world's probable verdict on him.

It goes without saying that the verdict was in each case favourable. The respect due to distinguished public figures was enhanced by the belief that they had met —"in what circumstances one shudders to think"—the deaths of martyr-heroes; the writers (or writer?) contrive with unobtrusive craftsmanship to animate what seems to us a stilted prose with the throb of emotions which were shared by an outraged and sorrowing nation.

But in arriving at those verdicts the evidence is set out with objectivity and interpreted with percipience; and when, some two months later, the three men were able to peruse these memorials, two of them must, I think, have found between the lines implications which gave them food for thought.

During Sir Robert Hart's forty-six years in China, *The Times* noted, he had visited Europe only twice; for the last twenty-one years, save for one journey to Hongkong and two short visits to the seaside, he had not left Peking. Had it occurred to this cock on his Imperial dunghill that "in some respects his usefulness might have been greater if he had kept himself more in contact with the outer world"? *The Times* did not say that Hart was so much in the pocket of the Chinese that, as a local expert whose advice was automatically sought by successive British Ministers, he was a bit of a menace. It said: "The influence which he thus exercised over British policy cannot be said to have been wholly beneficial, for, in his uncompromising loyalty to those he served, he was bound to act above all, whether consciously or unconsciously, as their advocate and champion." Had this conception of the leading role he had played for so long in Peking ever presented itself to Sir Robert?

I wonder. We sometimes learn, with or without a

shock, what some people think of us at a given juncture. How often do we learn what everyone has thought about us for years?

There were (so to speak) fewer bones in Sir Claude MacDonald's kedgeree. But when he read that his appointment, after a successful tour of duty in West Africa, "to one of the most difficult and responsible posts in the diplomatic service . . . caused at the time widespread surprise," was he, too, a little bit surprised? Widespread surprise is frequently generated by appointments in every walk of life; but how many candid friends tell the appointed that everyone is dumbfounded by his superiors' choice? It is the sort of thing that only comes out in one's obituary.

Morrison's included no reservations. At thirty-eight he was the youngest of the obituarees; Sir Claude was forty-eight, Sir Robert sixty-five. He had only the years of achievement behind him; there was no question of the second or the third act disappointing. All sources combine to suggest that he had in his nature and his outlook on life that golden quality which I, on slight acquaintance, found in his son Ian, who met in Korea a death narrowly and rather often risked elsewhere as a War Correspondent of *The Times*.

Morrison's obituary is a fine but never a flowery tribute to a solitary adventurer who became a figure to reckon with in his country's affairs. Curzon's "now historic phrase about 'the intelligent anticipation of events before they occur' " was, *The Times* felt, "though not primarily intended as a compliment, perhaps the most genuine tribute ever wrung from unwilling lips to the highest qualities which a correspondent can bring to bear upon his work." Among the experiences which had qualified Morrison to earn this tribute were a transit of Australia on foot (2,043 miles in 123 days: "when he was overtaken by floods he waded and swam"): an expedition to New Guinea, where he was left for dead with two spears in his body: and a 3,000-mile walk from Shanghai to Burma which cost him £18.

One would like to think that he read his obituary with unmixed pleasure. But he was, as it pointed out, "essentially modest and unassuming"; and when, three months after it appeared, he wrote to Printing House Square "I shall never be able to live up to the reputation given me in your obituary of the 17th July," it is fair to assume that his words expressed a genuine misgiving.

You can, I suppose, at a pinch dine out on the fact that you have read your own obituary; but there is a rule that you cannot have the best of both worlds, and you were in the wrong world when you read it. I suspect that it pays, in this as in many other matters, to stick to the rules.

TV IDOL TELLS ALL

The bookcase was real, in so far as anything there could be so described, but the books in it were not. They were a *trompe-l'œil*, a black and white photostat of book-spines fitted into the shelves. This struck me as a practical arrangement. To a layman's eye a couple of sensitive characters from the Real Book Shifters Union would not have swollen perceptibly the crowd of technicians on the studio floor: but their wages would have sent up the overheads, and their *raison d'être* would have involved an element of capital expenditure.

All the same, I could not help feeling that there was a slight lack of artistic integrity about the dummy book backs. Our panel game was supposed to be taking place in the chairman's flat in London's famed West End; a relaxed, convivial, intimate atmosphere was aimed at, and champagne was being served to foster it. It was real champagne, we sat huddled together in real armchairs and we were, up to a point, real people. I felt obscurely that this ha'porth of illusion was unworthy of the occasion.

This feeling was strengthened when I looked to see what books had been photostatted to provide our urbane conversation piece with a suitable background. Pettigrew on *The Gross Registered Ton, Some Aspects of Demurrage* by Craik and Fowle, V. J. Bearcraft's *Tabulation of Efficiency Quotients in the Jute Industry*, Gadsden's *The Recurring Decimal in Health and Sickness*—these actual titles may not have been among those which met my eye; but all the books were, or had been, that *sort* of book.

Around the cameras, the microphones and the other apparatus a large posse of technicians, awaiting H-hour, combed their hair and bestowed on the assembled panel those thumbs-down-but-good-luck-to-you looks which one sees round the paddock when a small field is saddling up for the Ladies' Race on a cold Saturday in March.

A girl in a white kennel coat appeared and asked me to follow her to the make-up room. I protested. I said that I had done this sort of thing before and we hadn't had to be made up then.

"I can't help that," she replied. "For this programme you have to be. Just a light make-up."

In no time at all she had me in a surplice and was slapping the greasepaint on to my face.

"Hey, steady!" I said. "I don't want all that stuff on."

She said not to worry, she was just toning me down; my face was the wrong colour.

What did she mean, the wrong colour?

She said it was sort of *brown*.

"But good heavens!" I cried. "Lots of people have brown faces. Millions, in fact. What do you do when you have an Indian on television?"

She said Indians were different and got to work on my ears. A strong mutual antipathy had arisen between us.

When she had finished I looked as if I was suffering from jaundice and pernicious anæmia and had not much longer to live. I made my way to an empty dressing-room and scraped the stuff off with a handkerchief. There were still a few minutes before we were due on the air. I went out into the mean alleys behind the old music hall and lit a pipe.

Twilight was only just beginning to fall, and after a bit I noticed that people eyed me curiously as they hurried past on their way home. I knew they couldn't be mistaking me for Mr. Richard Dimbleby and began to suspect that my endeavours to remove the make-up had gone amiss; so I sought once more the mirror in the empty dressing-room and gazed earnestly at my face.

It looked perfectly normal; and in the bustle which heralded our appearance before an audience of long-suffering millions I had no time to speculate further about what it was in my appearance which had attracted the wondering, almost startled glances of the passers-by.

Afterwards, shepherded back into the make-up room with the rest of the panel, I met with a feeling of guilt the beady eye of the girl whose efforts I had sabotaged.

"I don't really think——" I began when she proffered unguents and paper towels.

"Just as you like," she said. The faintly complacent note in her voice made me look into the triptych mirror on the dressing-table; and in it I saw that my swarthy features were flanked by a pair of primrose-coloured ears.

I have appeared infrequently on television. There are several good reasons for this, but probably the most cogent is that when I appear that is all I do; I just appear.

"Ha! Ha!" says the master of ceremonies. "I must say, that's just about the best reason I ever heard for not eating water-melons by moonlight. Thank you very much, Major. Now, er, Strix. You must have been involved in some equally odd predicaments in the course of your varied career. Would you like to——"

While the master of ceremonies is saying "Would you like to," I have begun saying "Well, er, as a matter of fact, I don't honestly think." He stops talking because he believes that at last I am going to say something; I stop talking because I realise that I have rudely interrupted him.

This brings the sound part of the programme temporarily to a close. The cut and thrust of debate is interrupted, there is a loss of tempo, and the viewers are back in the old days of the silent film. If I am on the top of my form they can see me crossing one leg over the other with a well-meaning but *désorienté* air before the cameras switch back to the master of ceremonies.

"Perhaps," he says, with just a touch of petulance, "we had better get on to the next question." As he says this viewers can hear my voice, like a seagull making background noises in an over-produced nautical drama, mumbling, "All I was going to say was that I don't think I've got anything to——"

I made my television début in 1938. The programme was, as I remember, a short one for those days and lasted only three-quarters of an hour. It consisted basically of a soliloquy by me on the Sino-Japanese war. This was enlivened (perhaps it would be truer to say that artificial respiration was applied) by a nice man who drew with extraordinary cleverness and celerity maps illustrating my strategical expositions. Viewers were then so few that television was perfectly respectable but rather abstruse: like, today, growing mushrooms or breeding Shetland ponies. In an attempt to make my talk more vivid I began with a statement to the effect that "By the time you wake up tomorrow some hundreds if not thousands of Chinese men, women and children will, if the weather is favourable, have been killed or wounded by the Japanese Air Force."

In those days scripts dealing with any aspect of foreign affairs had to be submitted to the Foreign Office; and the Foreign Office, not wishing to give offence to the Japanese, put a blue pencil through this sentence. But it is one thing to censor a typescript and another to stop its author saying what he intends to say; and I am afraid I treated Mr. Neville Chamberlain's foreign policy in the same way as I treated the make-up.

I think that must have been almost the last occasion when I actually finished a sentence on television. I do as a matter of fact remember finishing one on the Brains Trust two or three years ago. Mrs. Mole of Skegness had written to report that her son Thomas, aged sixteen, always put his shirt on before his trousers, but that her husband, Mr. Mole, insisted that the trousers should be given priority over the shirt. What did the panel think?

I did not even wait to see what my colleagues—the scientist, the philosopher, the distinguished Indian lady —would make of this contemporary dilemma. I blurted out, "What an absolutely fatuous question!"

It was my finest hour. I was (quite rightly) not asked to appear on the Brains Trust again.

THE ELEPHANT AND THE LARKS

THE headline in a French local paper read:

UN CHASSEUR CHARENTAIS
MEURT D'ÉMOTION
AUPRÈS DU LIÈVRE
QU'IL VENAIT D'ABATTRE

I was musing on the affecting scene which these words conjured up when the *Daily Telegraph*'s account of a pheasant-shoot in California caught my eye. Three thousand guns, standing shoulder to shoulder, took part; 800 birds were "released"; one of the sportsmen, leaving the mêlée with six pellets in his face, made, for an American, a creditable approach to understatement by declaring "It's unsafe out there."

In matters connected with the chase the British, while admiring the often uncanny prowess of primitive peoples, have always regarded the foreign sportsman as slightly ridiculous and potentially dangerous. We respect and even marvel at the pigmy with his blow-pipe, the Kirghiz horseman with an eagle on his wrist, the aboriginal with his boomerang; but at the American hunter, with his bright, deterrent hat and his elaborate outfit by Abercrombie and Fitch, or at the Continental *chasseur* or *jäger*, slung about with musical instruments, given to rodomontade and libations to St. Hubert, and accompanied by strange, unruly dogs, we look down our noses. That one of them should fall dead with emotion after shooting a hare seems to us the most natural thing in the world.

This snooty attitude on our part is unjust and unbecoming; but no one can deny that the behaviour and the attitude of foreigners engaged in field sports is, very often, different from ours, and that these differences, whether marked or subtle, offer a fruitful field for sociological if not for ethnological study.

I remember a few years ago walking back from a rabbit-shoot with two of the other guns: one, an Englishman, was an old friend, the other, who was Italian by birth, a new friend.

I noticed for the first time that the Englishman had a plug of cottonwool or something of the sort in one ear, and asked him why. He explained that he always plugged that ear when he was shooting; it had been damaged years ago when somebody had fired over his shoulder at a charging elephant.

"What a curious thing!" said the Italian. "I too damaged one ear out shooting. In Italy we used to dig pits in the ground and put little bits of mirror round the edge. Then we hid in the pits and the glitter attracted the birds. I was walking close to a pit which I thought was empty when the man inside it, who had not seen me, fired and the detonation injured my ear-drum."

"But what were the birds?" we asked.

"Larks," said the Italian.

Except for Welsh miners and the Corps of Royal Engineers, the British are basically rather afraid of high explosive; their attitude to it, which is one of non-involvement and distrust, approximates to the alleged attitude of foreigners to soap, as depicted by late Victorian humorists. This is probably one of the reasons why they handle their firearms with scrupulous care and are horrified by the happy-go-lucky methods in vogue elsewhere. An apocryphal story of my youth described a *nouveau riche* bringing his shooting party into the house for luncheon: "All on safe, chaps!" he cried, as he thrust his gun into the umbrella-stand. I suspect that many foreigners, while appreciating that to put a gun in the umbrella-stand was a droll solecism, might miss the real point of the story, which is the iniquity of taking a loaded gun indoors at all. Last week, I see, the original head of the Gestapo was killed while extricating his loaded gun from a car; accidents from this cause are common in America.

In the matter of costume there is a further divergence of outlook. The British tradition, such as it is, implies that shooting is merely an extension of a man's normal activities; current American trends, to judge from the advertisements, suggest that a duck-hunt is only one degree less rugged than a journey into Outer Space; and on the Continent there is a weakness for what the Briton, conveniently forgetting the panoply of the hunting-field *chez lui*, is apt to deride as fancy dress.

In America the seasons for all types of game are short, and in most if not all States there are drastic legal restrictions on the number of head you can kill. I don't know what the wardrobe and equipment of a fully accoutred American sportsman costs, but it must be rather a lot in relation to the number of times in a year he is able to use it.

The Continental sportsman is more catholic in his choice of quarry than we are. A friend of mine who attended a rather grand shooting party in France earlier this month told me that they got 800 head in four days, but that this total included a fairly large number of blackbirds. I asked if they shot thrushes too.

"Not now," he said. "There practically aren't any left. They're rather a delicacy in those parts."

Although in this country we eat the game we kill, the image of the pot is further from our minds than it is from the foreign sportsman's. In France the universal fusillade which greets the appearance of a hare is due only partly to the fact that some Frenchmen are excitable and "jealous" shots; it is due also to the fact that, where the Englishman sees a rather despised quadruped lolloping away from him, the Frenchman sees an appetising *terrine*. In some ways this semi-gastronomic approach to venery seems to me to reflect credit on the foreign sportsman.

In these islands shooting is, broadly speaking, an end in itself, and such perquisites as fresh air, exercise and scenery are all part of that end. In some countries other perquisites, less integral to the object of the exercise, are given a high value, and shooting is made the excuse, not only for dressing up, but for other subsidiary activities, of which perhaps the commonest is drinking. This particular tradition is much honoured in Russia, and on a shooting expedition which I once made in the Caucasus drink or its after-effects delayed the start of virtually every day's operations by about two hours. Though not one to refuse a glass of sloe gin after luncheon in a draughty barn in November, I do not think the Demon Alcohol can with advantage be given an important role in a day's shooting.

I feel I am safe in conjecturing that 90 per cent. of my readers know nothing about shooting and that 75 per cent. of them disapprove of it. This large majority will be justified in assuming that the British sportsman's attitude to his alien *confrères* is insular and overweening, and what I have written will strengthen their conviction that anyone who shoots must be a boor and a Philistine, if nothing worse. I am afraid there is nothing I can do about this. But I have at least produced evidence to suggest that odd and untoward things do sometimes occur when the foreigner gets a fowling-piece into his hands.

THE OTHERNESS OF SNEED

I suppose that in almost every club there is a member who, though he uses the place a great deal, never really seems to *belong*. He is not exactly aloof; he is not mysterious; he does not give the impression of being shy. He is rather like the lizard on the wall of your bungalow in the tropics. Spread-eagled, brooding, inscrutable and vaguely proprietorial, liable at any moment to vanish none can say whither, to reappear none can say whence, the lizard produces a disturbing sensation of *otherness*; and it is rather the same with the type of member I have in mind.

There is one of the Culverin Club. I think his name is Sneed; I have always thought this. But I once heard him addressed as Fortescue by a member whom I do not know. "Good morning, Fortescue," said this chap as they passed each other in a doorway. "Good morning," replied (as I maintain) Sneed in a flat, ungracious voice; from the quick appraising glance which he gave the other you could deduce nothing. There was perhaps a flicker of surprise in it, but no more than you would expect from a man who, since he never speaks to anybody, is virtually never spoken to himself.

Most of us, if addressed *en passant* by the wrong name, tend to react in some positive way. We look blank, taken aback. We begin (even if we only begin) to expostulate by saying "Er" or "What?" or "As a matter of fact." We join a group of acquaintances and ask if anybody knows the tall man in glasses who has just left the room and who appears to believe that our name is Smethurst. We *do* something about it.

The fact that Sneed did nothing throws, in my view,

no light on what his name really is. This aura of otherness, this highly-developed capacity for appearing not to
belong, are perfectly compatible with the acceptance of
an alias, fortuitously bestowed. It is of course possible
that Fortescue is Sneed's Christian name; but the inherent improbability of anybody calling Sneed by his
Christian name is so great that I think we can rule out
this solution.

It must be five years or more since an incident occurred
in which Sneed's behaviour became, for the first and
as far as I know the last time, positively rather than
negatively enigmatic.

The other person involved was Dinmont, the distinguished actor. One morning he and Sneed were
sitting opposite each other on either side of the fireplace
in the reading room, looking through the illustrated
papers. At one o'clock or thereabouts Dinmont got up to
go into luncheon. As he did so Sneed put down the *Tatler*,
directed at his fellow-member a searching glance, and
spoke.

"I see," he said, "that you've put your socks on
today, Dinmont." The words were uttered on a note of
grudging approval.

"I'm sorry," said Dinmont, unable to believe his
ears, "but *what* did you say?"

Sneed repeated his observation.

Dinmont felt slightly out of his depth. "Of course I've
put my socks on," he said. "What do you expect? I
always wear socks."

"You were not wearing socks the other day," replied
Sneed darkly.

"What on earth do you mean?" Dinmont was getting
rather annoyed. "When wasn't I wearing them?"

"Last Tuesday," said Sneed. "In here. I saw
you."

"But look here," said Dinmont, "a man can't *forget* to put on his socks."

"I never said you forgot," Sneed pointed out. He picked up the *Tatler* again.

"But damn it all," cried Dinmont, nettled and bemused, "are you suggesting that I'm the sort of chap who deliberately goes about London without any socks on?"

"I'm not suggesting anything," Sneed replied. "All I said was that you had put your socks on this morning. It's perfectly true. I can't see them now that you are standing up, but I could when you were sitting opposite me. Surely there's no need for you to get cross?"

At this point Dinmont, who is an equable man with a good sense of humour, realised that this insane argument might go on for ever. Muttering something about having to lunch early, he broke contact and made for the dining room.

He happened to sit next to me (this is a true story, by the way) and lost no time in telling me of his experience. He explained that it had already begun to assume a dream-like quality in his mind and that he was anxious to pass on a first-hand account to someone else before his memories of what had passed between him and Sneed dissolved or became distorted.

We agreed that to commend a man for wearing socks in his club was a subtler form of character-assassination than asking him if he had stopped beating his wife. Dinmont admitted that he felt seriously disconcerted by the allegation that he had not been wearing socks on the previous Tuesday. He knew it was not true and maintained that it could not be true, being against nature; it was, he reasoned, a physical impossibility to omit a *penultimate* process when dressing. You could put on a shirt and forget to put on a tie, but you couldn't put on a tie and forget to put on a shirt. By the same token (argued Dinmont, whose whole intellect was by now working on the problem with a feverish vigour) you couldn't, however absentminded you were, stuff your bare feet into a pair of shoes without noticing that something was wrong.

I said I agreed with all this, but why had Sneed broken his customary silence to make the strange allegation?

"I only wish I knew," muttered Dinmont, eating smoked salmon with a hunted air. "It isn't the sort of charge that you'd think a man would fabricate, even if he had a motive for doing so. In a way that's what makes it so disturbing. I can't *prove* that I was wearing socks last Tuesday. I can't even say that I remember putting my socks on, because one does that sort of thing automatically."

"You could appeal for witnesses," I suggested.

"But nobody sees your socks," said Dinmont, "unless you happen to sit down in an armchair, which I hardly ever do. Besides, think what a fool I should look if the secretary put up a notice asking anyone who can vouch for the fact that I was wearing socks last Tuesday to get in touch with him. People would think I was going round the bend." There was a distraught note in his voice.

"You mustn't let this get you down," I said. "The important thing is to watch for Sneed's next move. He's bound to show his hand sooner or later. When he does, we shall know how to act."

Sneed has not shown his hand. For five years Dinmont and I and one or two others have kept him under observation. When opportunity offers we carry the war into the enemy's country by directing casual but pregnant glances at his socks. But our expectation that he would strike again has proved groundless. He seems to have relapsed into otherness.

Once, about two years ago, a report reached us which seemed to indicate that this front might be reactivated, that the lizard on the wall was about to abandon the *couchant regardant* for some more positive posture. Sneed, having polished off his Irish stew, was heard to order an ice.

"Certainly, sir," said the waitress. "What kind would you like? Chocolate?"

Sneed gave her a furious, affronted look.

"Chocolate!" he barked. "*Certainly not!*"

But when they brought him a vanilla ice he ate it up like a lamb. He remains an enigma.

HELLO THERE, BARON FUKUSHIMA!

I HAD completely forgotten about Baron Fukushima. Yet there he is in the front row, seated in a vaguely simian posture next to Major the Reverend J. C. Chute and clutching in his white-gloved paws an enormous sword.

Now I come to think of it, there was a sort of minor plague of Japanese notabilities during my last year at Eton. The present Emperor, then Crown Prince, paid us a visit, and when he took his departure Lord Hailsham and I had the invidious task of leading the entire school in a deep-throated roar of "Sayonara!", which is Japanese for "Farewell!" Lord Hailsham and I were, of course, word-perfect; but Etonians have never been demonstrative, and many of our fellow pupils expressed their disapproval of what they felt to be a rather fulsome ceremony by departing from the authorised version and bawling "Toodle-oo!", "Any old iron?", "Six to four the field!" and other expressions of an even more inappropriate kind. I thought His Imperial Highness looked a shade baffled as the deep-throated roar died away.

Baron Fukushima looks a bit baffled too. I do not find this surprising, for it is clear on internal evidence that he has just witnessed the annual inspection of the Eton College OTC by General Sir G. F. Milne, GCMG, KCB, DSO, who occupies the centre of the front row. I am sure that our evolutions were carried out with the customary dash and precision, but there is (or there was in those days) a *je ne sais quoi* about the Corps which might well have engendered perplexity in the scion of a warrior-race.

Except for P. V. F. Cazalet, who wears an expression of astonished indignation, and Captain and Quartermaster H. K. Marsden, who has a lycanthropic crouch and seems to be about to hurl himself on the photographer and tear out his throat with long, sharp teeth, the rest of us merely look glazed. The photograph is headed "E.C.O.T.C. Officers and Sergeants 1926." There are forty-nine of us, counting the Baron.

Taking the age of the boys in this group as eighteen, and assuming that they went to their private schools when they were nine years old, I calculate that the average number of group-photographs in which each had up till then featured was round about thirty. For a good all-round athlete the figure would be higher. The eleven-year-old who makes his début squatting on the ground in front of the First XI is going to be constantly before the camera through the ensuing years, and by the end of his University career will have accumulated enough stuff to fill a small picture gallery. What happens to all this junk?

Junk may seem an over-disparaging term to apply to what are in a sense hard-won trophies. It is however scarcely possible that a lower art-form than the group-

185

photograph exists. Unless you happen either to have been or to have begotten one of them, a picture of eleven stony-faced louts and a football is not a picture that can be contemplated with pleasure; and when, as often happens, it hangs beside another picture depicting eight of the original louts with three new recruits the effect is painfully monotonous.

Nor can its possessor derive any very lively satisfaction from it. He may, when he was first given his colours, have gloated in private over the bright, new, long-coveted cap; but he does not feast his eyes on the photograph of the First XI, indeed once he has hung it on his wall he practically never looks at it again. It would be different if he had won a point-to-point and had framed a photograph of his horse getting its nose in front over the last fence; that picture, immortalising an event, a crisis, and deriving beauty and urgency from the horses, would give him enjoyment whenever he saw it, and he would like other people to see it too. The group, even in the lavatory, is merely a waste of wall-space.

I suspect that it is often Mum who starts the rot by initially encouraging a trend from which she will be the chief sufferer in the long run ("Darling, do you *really* want me to get the glass mended? It's not a bit good of you, and it's only the *Second* XI"). When George comes home after his first term and she finds in his trunk a photograph showing the pupils and staff at Otis Court huddled in a great, grey, blancmange-shaped phalanx, she shows or simulates an eager curiosity.

Here, she first thinks, is something that ought to get him talking; for she longs to break through the silence-barrier, to tear aside the veil of polite taciturnity behind which the infant has hidden the decisive and doubtless alarming experiences of the last three months. The photograph proves useless for this purpose. "*He* looks

186

rather nice. Is he a friend of yours?" "*No.*" "Isn't this
the boy who was in the next bed when you all had 'flu?"
"*Yes.*" "What's he like?" "*Not bad.*"

Stalemated here, she turns to the idea—widely pre-
valent among ladies whose first male child has just
returned from boarding-school—of buttressing his status
as a Big Boy. She believes that this purpose will be
furthered by having the school photograph framed and
hung in his room; and she is influenced in this by the
undoubted fact that the interior decoration of a bedroom
occupied by a small boy presents problems of taste which
are not easily solved in the early stages. So up it goes—
"Otis Court, 1957"—the first of a long series in its deadly
genre.

Nobody can prevent these photographs being taken.
It would be wrong if anybody tried to. They have, in the
school, the athletic club or the regimental depot, the
status of archives; and occasionally, when some dim
man goes berserk in Patagonia or makes mincemeat of his
mistress in Moulmein, they help our great national newspapers to discharge their duty to the reading public.

But this in no way lessens the administrative problems
connected with their display, disposal and storage. The
only helpful suggestion I can offer is based on my
fortuitous re-encounter with Baron Fukushima and my
other, closer comrades-in-arms, which has given me true
though abstruse pleasure. This is that group-photographs should be laid down like pipes of port, and concealed among the general detritus of a household so
effectively that they will not be seen again for a minimum
of thirty years.

If, indeed, ever.

ALLEGED NATION

SPEAKING for the trades union movement the other day, Mr. Frank Cousins observed: "It might be said, 'Why do we not co-operate with the Government?' There are two simple reasons. One, they have never asked us; and, secondly, they would never have us if we offered because they do not want to develop productivity."

These are the saddest words I ever heard.

This may seem a large claim to make; and it is quite true that, like everyone else of my years, I have at one time or another listened to more poignant utterances. But they were wrung from individuals, speaking for themselves under stress or in anguish; and what these people said, though it may have been heart-rending or at least pathetic, was not what I mean here by sad. In me Mr. Cousins's words induced a sort of vast, flat, grey, November-Sunday-afternoon-in-Manchester sorrow.

To prove his second reason valid would require casuistry of a high order; but any lawyer of moderate skill could readily show that his first complaint was well founded.

"And have you, Mr. Cousins, ever received—personally, I mean—a written or oral communication from any one of Her Majesty's Ministers inviting you to co-operate in any form of effort or enterprise ostensibly designed for the national benefit?"

"No."

"It has been suggested, with what may fairly be called tedious iteration, that you, as an alert and responsible trades union leader, might have interpreted as applying in some sense to yourself and to your members the frequent appeals made by representatives of all three parties, and by every organ of the press except the *Daily Worker*, to the population as a whole. The burden of these exhortations was, if I may lapse into nautical idiom, 'All hands to the pumps!' Am I right in saying that, in so far as you were aware of these expressions of opinion, you felt fully justified in disregarding them?"

"Yes."

"My client, m'lud, is a busy man. The court has heard that no direct approach was made to him from any authoritative quarter in regard to the alleged economic crisis from which our alleged nation is, according to hearsay, suffering. Is it reasonable that a man so unsparing of his energies, a man so closely involved in the direction of important affairs, a man with (to use a colloquialism) so much on his plate—is it reasonable that such a man should be expected to assimilate, let alone to act upon, a succession of trite and arbitrary appeals made to his fellow-citizens—latterly for the most part by individuals of whom he does not approve—to put national before sectional interests in an emergency?"

Perhaps I am being unfair to Mr. Cousins, of whom I know nothing but who appears (to those who do not know him) to share the resolution, the testiness and the congenital myopia of the other larger pachyderms. He is clearly no fool and he must have integrity, otherwise— *pace* Horatio Bottomley and Hitler—he would not be where he is. All I do know is that, when he spoke the words quoted at the beginning of this article, he set a bad example and helped to perpetuate a bad state of affairs in this country.

Our current dilemma stems from this: that the British have somehow got themselves into the position of supplying both the actors and the audience for an endless season of old-fashioned, artificial and intrinsically almost worthless plays. Suez momentarily brought the whole theatre to life; it was as though Shakespeare had suddenly written a scene into some stilted, stumbling tragicomedy by Dekker. The actors whipped out their convictions and had at each other like mad, before the bright dew could rust their blades; the empurpled audience cheered or booed with frenzy. It was not a savoury interlude; it was far from being a desirable norm; and it did not have a happy ending. But at least, for once, the actors spoke direct to the audience; and the audience, briefly paroled from the dull, unreal, imperfectly understood conventions of contemporary political drama, could feel something, could participate, could choose for themselves their own heroes and their own villains.

Now we are back in the rut, lounging and yawning in our Welfare State stalls. On the stage the actors grimace and rant and attitudinise. Flimsy, elaborate pretences are maintained. When the Socialists call the Tories blackguards whose sole aim in life is to harry the old-age pensioners and enrich the landlords, or when the Tories denigrate the Socialists in terms almost equally extravagant, the audience is expected to take this fustian seriously.

But we don't. The suspension of disbelief is not achieved. In a real theatre we are well prepared to accept the convention that a Shakespearian heroine, perfunctorily disguised in doublet and hose, is totally unrecognisable to her nearest and dearest. But on the political stage these shallow and obsolete impostures no longer earn indulgence on our side of the footlights. The insistence of each faction that its opponents' motives are invariably base and their policies inevitably misguided, though apparently indispensable to the conduct of the drama, strikes most sensible people as plain silly.

This quality of silliness is not the prerogative of any party, but it has seldom been better illustrated than by

190

those words of Mr. Cousins which I have quoted. It is not so much their childish content that saddens as the fact that up there, on the stage, they are accepted as a legitimate and telling piece of dialogue. We no longer go to the real theatre to hear the players bellow, "Dead! And never called me mother!" or try to curdle our blood with references to a fate worse than death. In that other, larger, theatre, where we are a captive audience and cannot ask for our money back, we can scarcely be blamed if we watch the performances of the repertory company with a growing listlessness.

In some quarters, I suspect, apathy is sharpening into impatience, if not into disgust. The political actors now come, thanks to television, closer to the audience than of yore, yet they seem more remote than ever. The Government and the Opposition, the besieged and the besiegers, are straitly confined within their party lines. Since the central defences, rigid yet infinitely elaborate, will one day change hands, long sectors of the battlements and earthworks are virtually immune from attack. The opportunist saps and counter-scarps of the assailants are themselves inhibited in design by the need to conform, or to seem to conform, to the pattern of a threadbare and half-baked ideology to which its warmest adherents pay, at best, only a frothy lip-service. And from the ever-smouldering camp fires and the small, booming guns of both sides rises a gritty pall of unnecessary animosities and provocations; through it, emblazoned on the rival banners, can scarcely be descried slogans which, when they have any meaning at all, appear to be almost identical.

On many of its spectators this scene produces a depressing effect. The British are, by and large, a united, resourceful and fair-minded nation. The main reason why in the past they survived so many perils and overcame so many difficulties is that they did not in a crisis wait to be "asked" to do something about it; and as they watch this protracted, profitless, unreal siege of one party by another, they cannot help wondering for how much longer the niceties and the nonsense of a *Kriegspiel* are going to sour the air, distort the nation's image and keep us, firmly, in the red.